"If leadership is about influence, then, after Jesus, Mary was the greatest leader of all time. Uniquely, she was present at the three great moments of our redemption: the incarnation, passion, and pentecost. In this book, Amy Orr-Ewing presents Mary's perspective—her fear, her faith, and her wisdom—to highlight how her life can offer hope to all who journey through tears, disappointment, lament, struggle, and pain."

—Nicky and Pippa Gumbel, author, pioneers of Alpha, and Vicar of Holy Trinity Brompton, London

"What better companions could there possibly be for our journey through Advent to Christmas than these two women: Mary, the mother of Jesus, who speaks more powerfully into this season than any other, and Amy Orr-Ewing, a trusted voice and respected friend whose insights never fail to encourage and inspire me"

—Pete Greig, founder of 24-7 Prayer International and senior pastor of Emmaus Rd Church

"A beautiful and intensely thoughtful set of Christmas reflections, given added depth by a stunning set of illustrations."

—Professor Alister McGrath, University of Oxford

"In *Mary's Voice: Advent Reflections to Contemplate the Coming of Christ*, Amy helps us to recapture the awe and wonder of the birth of Christ and what this means for us today. By elevating the voice of the young, strong, vulnerable, marginalized, courageous, obedient, faithful, and often overlooked, Mary, the mother of God, Amy unveils profound insights into the meaning of Christmas. This book will be a great companion as you prepare your heart during the Advent season. I have never been more captivated by Advent reflections and know you will see Jesus more clearly and love him more dearly as you journey through these pages."

—Christine Caine, founder of A21 and Propel Women

"Rich, deeply beautiful, and moving, *Mary's Voice* shows why Christmas, for all its fevered rush and consumerism, is still the festival that slows the racing mind, stills the overloaded heart, and creates wonder. Amy's meditations deepen our understanding and sympathy for Mary, for Advent, and for all women, too, but in a way that also makes her reflections rich for men and for all who seek for the meaning of life."

—Os Guinness, author of *The Call*

"Looking through the lens of a woman in the twenty-first century about a woman in the first century, *Mary's Voice* is unlike any Advent devotional I've ever read. Amy Orr-Ewing compels her readers to consider Mary's "enormity of responsibility" in the longing and waiting of the coming King. Capturing my heart into the wonder of the incarnation through the life and perspective of Mary, I know this book will make an impact in the lives of women for many more centuries to come."

—Rev. Lisa Wink Schultz, chief of staff,
US Senate Chaplain's Office

"In *Mary's Voice*, Amy has provided a beautiful and unique perspective surrounding Christ's birth. This devotional opened my eyes to a new way of imagining that first Christmas through Mary's eyes. What a gift!"

—Lauren McAfee, founder, Stand for Life, ministry director,
Hobby Lobby Ministry Investments

"As both a Christian and a pastor, I'm always looking for fresh insights, perspectives, and inspiration when considering the glory of the incarnation. Amy Orr-Ewing has provided all of that in her book *Mary's Voice*. A refreshing journey through the days of Advent with Mary, the mother of Jesus, as our guide. I loved it and am sure you will, too."

—Brian Brodersen, pastor, Calvary Chapel,
Costa Mesa, California

MARY'S
Voice

MARY'S

Voice

*Advent Reflections
to Contemplate
the Coming of Christ*

AMY ORR-EWING

Nashville • New York

Worthy

Hachette Book Group

1290 Avenue of the Americas, New York, NY 10104

worthypublishing.com

twitter.com/worthypub

First edition: October 2023

Published in association with Joy Eggerichs Reed of Punchline Agency

Worthy is a division of Hachette Book Group, Inc. The Worthy name and logo are trademarks of Hachette Book Group, Inc.

The publisher is not responsible for websites (or their content) that are not owned by the publisher.

Worthy Books may be purchased in bulk for business, educational, or promotional use. For information, please contact your local bookseller or the Hachette Book Group Special Markets Department at special.markets@ hbgusa.com.

Library of Congress Cataloging-in-Publication Data has been applied for.

ISBNs: 9781546004523 (hardcover), 9781546004547 (ebook)

Printed in China

WAI

10 9 8 7 6 5 4 3 2

For my parents, Hartmut and Jane,
in honor of your love and faithfulness

Contents

*Introduct*ion	xi	December 15	98
		December 16	105
December 1	1	December 17	112
December 2	8	December 18	118
December 3	15	December 19	125
December 4	22	December 20	131
December 5	29	December 21	137
December 6	35	December 22	144
December 7	42	December 23	151
December 8	49	December 24	158
December 9	56	December 25	166
December 10	63		
December 11	70	*Afterword*	173
December 12	77	*Acknowledgments*	181
December 13	84		
December 14	91		

INTRODUCTION

Imagine being a young woman in a forgotten corner of an occupied country oppressed by a powerful empire. Imagine being a woman at a time when a woman's voice meant nothing. And now, think for a moment about Mary, the mother of Jesus.

In the Christian story, Mary is the one who God chose to be the mother of Jesus.

In the run-up to Christmas, there is a peculiar amount of work to be done that might fall into the category of "physical and emotional labor." This is the endless, unseen work of caring that generally, if not exclusively, often falls to women. Despite all the advances in opportunity and equality in our society, women appear to carry the brunt of domestic and emotional labor. At Christmastime, it would be all too easy to exhaust ourselves further after the work, turmoil, trauma, and anxiety of the year that has just passed.

Centering a woman's perspective at Christmas is about far more than empathizing with the eye-watering feats of planning that go into pulling off seasonal festivities. Paying heed to a woman's viewpoint is necessary if we are going to truly celebrate Christmas, because the central character of the Christmas story, other than the baby Jesus, is a woman named Mary.

At Christmastime we remember that an ordinary, young,

poor, oppressed woman was chosen to play a significant and breakthrough role in the redemption of the world. Evil would be crushed and defeated through her seed. Her body was to play a part in showing the world that Jesus really is Emmanuel—*God with us*. Her theological insights and reactions are recorded for us in the New Testament.

By positioning Mary in this way, the New Testament is unlike any document of the era. We can see what kind of person is invited to be a gospel witness, a teacher of profound theology, and an example of simple, humble faith. It is no mistake that a woman gets to be a part of all this, and that her voice, her questions, her fears, her actions, and her obedience matter.

The Christmas story accentuates one woman's perspective. Her fear, her faith, and her wisdom form an astonishing aspect of the story of how God became a person for the love of this world, and how Jesus of Nazareth on that first Christmas Day could be called "*the Son of God*." And in our weary world that is waiting and longing for light, meaning, peace, and love, perhaps we might do as Mary did when she "*treasured up all these things and pondered them in her heart*."

We first encounter Mary as a young unmarried teenager, but for many of us she remains fixed in our imaginations as a remote "other worldly" figure, with the faint glimmer of a smile talking to an angel or holding a baby. Held up by some as the unattainable ideal of purity or the example of perfect motherhood, Mary is a distant figure for us in our busy lives in this technological age. In our reading and telling of the events surrounding the birth of Jesus Christ, Mary's point of view is seldom considered. In the many re-enactments of the nativity story around Christmastime, Mary is usually a mute figure, saying nothing as the story of the journey to Bethlehem, the search for accommodation, and the birth of the child surrounded by animals unfolds. We may be familiar with the star of Bethlehem, the manger as a cradle, the shepherds, the angels, and the visit of the Magi. Portrayals of the nativity abound, but amidst it all Mary is a passive and silent figure. I once played the role of Mary in a school play, and for the entire show I did not utter a word.

Yet Mary is described in Luke's gospel as a woman who exercised choice, questioned things, reflected, responded, spoke up, and demonstrated great faith. Mary had a voice.

I can remember exactly where I was when I was first truly struck by Mary's voice. I had slipped into a pew in one of Britain's most beautiful cathedrals on a Wednesday at dusk for evensong. I was chilled to the bone in the moment of the service when the choir sang the words of Mary's Magnificat recorded for us in Luke's gospel: "*He hath put down the mighty from their seats, and exalted them of low degree.*"

I had spent that day sitting in the public gallery of a court supporting someone who was giving evidence in a criminal trial concerning childhood abuse. Mary's words expressing hope on behalf of the poor, the humble, and the powerless felt especially meaningful that evening in the aftermath of the horrors of trauma recounted in that courtroom. Until this point, Mary had been a somewhat remote figure for me. A woman often depicted wearing blue clothing in paintings, idealized as the perfect mother of a cherubic baby. Mary was stuck in my mind in suspended animation in the early stages of her motherhood, holding a baby and remembered each year as a rather distant figure when Christmas rolled around. Yet here was Mary's voice, her actual words recorded in Luke's gospel, prophesying about what Jesus had come to do, identifying Jesus as God, Lord, and the source of justice and mercy in this world. Mary had offered theological insights and shared her unique perspective on the person of Jesus Christ. Her front-row seat on history had somehow passed me by. But I realized in that moment that Mary's voice is worth listening to.

It seems that Luke (the author of the Gospel of Luke) did exactly that; he listened. At the start of his gospel narrative, he shares his method in writing: *"since I myself have carefully investigated everything from the beginning, I too decided to write an orderly account…"* (Luke 1:3). Luke was a doctor—a man of science and learning. He was also a gentile. He had not lived through or experienced firsthand the life and ministry of Jesus. So when he wrote his gospel he needed to go and interview the key eyewitnesses to the life of Jesus, and to investigate the history. He explains to his readers that he adopted this methodology intentionally: *"so that you may know the certainty of the things you have been taught"* (Luke 1:4). It mattered to Luke that we, his readers, could know for certain that the accounts of Jesus's life are true, so that we could trust and be sure even though, like him, we don't have personal or direct experience of the events he records. And to achieve that he needed to go back to the beginning—and that meant going to listen to Mary.

Luke's gospel draws on Mary as the primary witness throughout his historical narrative. He is held up by scholars as particularly interesting because he draws so heavily on the experiences of women. Mary is the primary source of his information. And that is why Luke is able to give us such an intimate account of how the birth of Jesus came to be in his gospel. Mary's voice and perspective have been preserved for us. Luke doesn't merely include Mary in the story, he centers her perspective as our viewpoint into the story of how God came to be a human being. Dorothy L. Sayers called the incarnation "the greatest story ever told."[1] The creator enters his own world as a human being, and the author of life appears as a character in his own story. The primary witness to all of this is Mary.

Luke includes details of Mary's personal experience around the conception, pregnancy, and birth of Jesus that could only have come directly from her. She recounts interactions from this period with characters such as the shepherds, Elizabeth, Anna, Simeon, and of course Joseph. To have access to the direct speech and reactions of these key figures from history is astonishing and precious. We will take time to dwell on the meaning and significance of each as we journey through the book.

Mary's Voice will also explore the themes that were important to Mary as she pondered and reflected upon who Jesus really is. Mary's theology is deep, and her Christology—her understanding of Christ—matters greatly given her role as

---

1   Dorothy L. Sayers, "The Dogma Is the Drama," in *Creed or Chaos?* p. 24.

a firsthand witness to the events and as Jesus's mother. Her reflections upon the suffering of this world and the meaning of Jesus's arrival connect with all who journey through tears, disappointment, lament, struggle, and pain.

Mary also speaks about power—one of the biggest issues of our day—and her words remain as relevant to today as ever. She understands the longings of those who find themselves oppressed and points us to the one who *"fills the hungry with good things."* The central woman to the Christian faith has a voice, and she uses it to point us toward the Lord Jesus. Encouraging us to dwell on who he is and what he came into this world to do.

Mary's accounts have tremendous historical significance. The scriptures can give us a truly intimate account of how the birth of Jesus came to be, precisely because Mary's voice and insights have been preserved for us. It is worthwhile to take the time to dwell on the riches of her perspective. This matters at more than a literary or aesthetic level, although Mary's voice contributes to both. Because at the heart of the Christian faith is the claim that God entered his own creation in the person of Jesus Christ—the doctrine of the Incarnation—and the primary witness to the incarnation is Mary.

A woman's voice has been preserved for over two thousand years; this is something precious and profound in and of itself. But Mary shares with us *how* the arc of history has been shaped by the coming of God as a man. Her account is historical and detailed, but it is also laden with meaning and prophetic nuance. Mary's perspective is unique, profound, domestic, beautiful, good, and true. The earthiness and the wonder of the incarnation are both captured here.

And so, as Christmas rolls around again and another year passes, we have the opportunity to recapture some wonder as we remember the birth of Christ and to take time to reflect and dwell on the meaning of Jesus's birth. *Mary's Voice* is an invitation to prepare our hearts in a time called Advent, in anticipation of Christmas when we will celebrate and mark the birth of Christ into this world.

Advent means arrival. Traditionally, Christians have taken the days and weeks before Christmas Day to spiritually prepare hearts and minds to capture the theological wonder of the incarnation and to prepare for the second arrival of Jesus—his return. *Mary's Voice* is a journey through Advent driven by the theological insights of Mary, the mother of Jesus. This book begins on December 1 and accompanies the reader throughout Advent with daily spiritual preparation based on a passage of scripture, a reflection, and a visual image. The devotional draws on the voice and insights of one person who is absolutely central to the coming of God into the world, who may be seen but is rarely heard. This person is Mary; her voice, her wisdom, her theological insight, her praise, her reaction to the events—all of these are recorded for us in the gospels. *Mary's Voice* will help us as readers recapture the wonder of God's coming in history in the person of Jesus, through the lens of Mary's viewpoint, with daily theological reflections, poems, collections, and beautiful pictures.

At Advent, we have a unique opportunity to dwell daily

upon the marvelous truth that God became a human being and entered our world. God was born in history. In all the planning, preparing, partying, and organizing, don't forget to treasure the truth at the heart of Christmas primarily witnessed by a young woman. Jesus is Immanuel—*God with us*. In this world of pain, disappointment, exhaustion, and suffering the promise of Christmas is that a savior was born for us.

And maybe as you ponder all this in your heart, like Mary did, you will be able to experience the one who Isaiah prophesied would be the Prince of Peace. Charles Wesley finished his famous carol with that hope and I for one know I need it:

> *Hail the heaven-born Prince of Peace!*
> *Hail the Sun of Righteousness!*
> *Light and life to all he brings,*
> *risen with healing in his wings!*
> *Mild he lays his glory by,*
> *Born that man no more may die,*
> *Born to raise the sons of earth*
> *Born to give them second birth*
>
> Christmas Carol: "Hark! The Herald Angels
> Sing," Charles Wesley

Illustration from *The Book of Hours*,
Lambeth Palace Library, London.

The *Book of Hours* is an illustrated manuscript. It is a Flemish book handwritten in Latin for English use, and it was created on Vellum in the 1400s before the invention of paper. It is a devotional book that was used to pray at different points during the day, drawing from the psalms and including hymns and readings.

In this image Mary and Joseph are depicted inside the letter D, which stands for *Deus*—meaning God. They are kneeling before Christ as an infant, with a donkey and an ox drawing our attention to their humanity and earthiness. The simplicity of their context is a connection point for the viewer as the faces of Mary and Joseph are humble and strikingly human. All the faces (human and animal) turn outward from the page, beckoning us in invitation to join them in worship of Christ. The detail of the extended, decorative, floral frame of wildflowers, strawberries, and peonies echoes the praise of all creation. This image is one of hundreds as each page of the book has been intricately drawn.

MARY'S
Voice

*In the sixth month of Elizabeth's pregnancy, God sent the angel
Gabriel to Nazareth, a town in Galilee, to a virgin pledged
to be married to a man named Joseph, a descendant of David.
The virgin's name was Mary. The angel went to her and said,
"Greetings, you who are highly favored! The Lord is with you."*

*Mary was greatly troubled at his words and wondered what
kind of greeting this might be. But the angel said to her, "Do
not be afraid, Mary; you have found favor with God. You will
conceive and give birth to a son, and you are to call him Jesus.
He will be great and will be called the Son of the Most High.
The Lord God will give him the throne of his father David, and
he will reign over Jacob's descendants forever; his kingdom will
never end."*

*"How will this be," Mary asked the angel, "since I am a
virgin?"*

Luke 1:26–34

Consider for a moment what life might have been like for
a young woman in an insignificant district of an occupied country under the control of the most powerful
empire the world has ever known. And now contemplate the
experience of a woman at a time when a woman's voice meant
very little indeed; in fact, her testimony was practically worthless

in a court of law. Think of how a woman living under such oppression was also expected to follow the cultural norms of marriage. This is the world as Mary, the mother of Jesus, experienced it at the beginning of the first millennia.

Throughout this coming Advent season, I invite you to join me in reflecting upon Mary's perspective on the events surrounding the birth of Jesus the Son of God, considering what she thought, what she saw, what she witnessed, and what she came to believe. Luke draws on Mary as a primary eyewitness in his gospel, and he includes her unique experiences and responses. Luke centers Mary's perspective as our viewpoint into the story of how God came to be a human being.

In Luke 1, Mary receives this extraordinary message from an angelic visitor. She is a virgin; the text is clear that although she is betrothed to Joseph she had never slept with a man. The Angel Gabriel tells her that she is "*highly favored*" and that the Lord is "*with her.*" What a contrast with her situation on a natural level. Mary is poor, young, insignificant, female, and a citizen of an occupied people. God does not see our position, status, or potential as this world does with its hierarchies, priorities, and social delineations.

Mary is told that not only is she going to miraculously have a child, who will be "*the Son of the Most High*," but the child she will have will also be given David's throne. This meant that he was the heir to all the Old Testament prophecies about the Davidic line, and that he would be a visible ruler of the Jewish people. He would be God's Son, here on earth. The Angel Gabriel brings together the hopes of Israel here—that an anointed one, a Messiah, would come in the line of King David and deliver God's people with the promise that God himself would provide his own son for the salvation of all people.

Mary is given more detail—her son will not merely reign for a short time in history. He is not going to be a temporary savior for a particular moment of geopolitical difficulty that the Jewish nation finds itself in—Mary's son will be born in history *and* will reign forever.

Her son will be great and his "*kingdom will never end.*" The heart of the incarnation is captured in these words to Mary, which she in turn recounts to Luke. Her son, who will be born from her womb, her seed—her egg—and carried and then delivered from her body, will be such a great king that his kingdom will be eternal.

This is the wonder of the incarnation—the eternal God is born into history.

Luke reflects and records that Mary was worried when she heard this. She was troubled and she was afraid upon hearing those words. This is a reaction that rings true. The awesome revelation of who Jesus Christ is going to be—an eternal ruler who will be born in history—is given to a simple teenage girl. And quite naturally she is astonished.

Her question reflects her intelligence when she asks, "*How can this be since I am a virgin?*" Mary's question demonstrates that she did know how human biology worked. She understood the basics of reproduction. And she was prepared to speak up and question the angel. Biblical miracles and revelation happen in the real-world context that we experience, and so side by side with describing divine intervention the Bible is honest about our human questions, fear, and wonder when we are faced with something supernatural.

This capacity to grasp the revelation given to her says a lot about Mary, as does the enormity of the responsibility she is trusted with. But ultimately it says a lot about who our God is, including who he values and whose voice matters. Who gets to be a part of his purposes in this world? A young woman named Mary.

Reflect for a few minutes today on this moment in the Advent story. The promise given by an angel to a teenage girl is that God would come into human history through her womb and be born as a baby. Mary's child will be miraculously conceived, and when he is born, he is going to reign forever on David's throne.

Give thanks to God for his coming into this world, and as we look forward in our journey in Advent to discovering more of who Jesus is through the eyes of Mary, pray the words of a historic prayer that invites God to stir our hearts with faith and fruit for his kingdom.

PRAYER

Stir up we beseech thee, O Lord,
the wills of thy faithful people,
that they, plenteously bringing forth
the fruit of good works,
may of these be plenteously rewarded
through Jesus Christ our Lord. Amen.

The Church of England Book of Common Prayer

The Annunciation, Fra Angelico in the San Marco Monastery, Florence, Italy.

This fresco is one of a series of wall paintings by the monk Fra Angelico (1395–1455), and it can still be seen in the San Marco monastery in Florence, Italy. Many of his paintings, including another version of this subject, are on the bare walls of the bedrooms where the monks slept, and they remain pristine to this day. The open window with a space for kneeling echoes the sense of an encounter with God in simplicity, which was the hallmark of the original appearance and announcement of the conception of Jesus to Mary by the Angel Gabriel (known as the Annunciation).

The angel answered, "The Holy Spirit will come on you, and the power of the Most High will overshadow you. So the holy one to be born will be called the Son of God. Even Elizabeth your relative is going to have a child in her old age, and she who was said to be unable to conceive is in her sixth month. For no word from God will ever fail."

"I am the Lord's servant," Mary answered. "May your word to me be fulfilled." Then the angel left her.

Luke 1:35–38

Today on this Advent journey shaped by Mary's perspective, we consider the interaction between the Angel Gabriel and this unknown young girl living in an obscure part of an occupied land, where a defeated people labored under the control of a massive empire. This woman, Mary, heard the angel say to her, *"Don't be afraid; you have found favor with God, you will conceive and give birth to a son, and you are to call him Jesus, and He will be great, and he will be called the Son of the Most High."* What did Mary make of those words? The text says that she was afraid, and she was troubled and that she had asked *how* this could happen.

The angel replied that the Holy Spirit would come and that the very power of the Most High God would overshadow her.

Mary was a Jewish woman. She would have been steeped in the scriptures from childhood. She may have known the prophecy from Isaiah 7:14: "*Therefore the Lord himself will give you a sign: The virgin will conceive and give birth to a son, and he will call him Emmanuel.*"

It had been prophesied long ago in the history of her people that God was going to enter his own creation and be born of a virgin. God himself would be born as Emmanuel, which means "God with us." But it was never going to be an ordinary conception and birth. The sign signifying that God is at work in this way is that this child's birth is an intervention from outside—the Virgin will conceive and bring forth a child.

Mary may well have known those words of the prophet Isaiah, but she would certainly have known the words of Genesis 3:15, where her foremother Eve had been promised in the scriptures that her seed, the seed of the woman, would crush the serpent's head.

I will put enmity
Between you and the woman,
And between your seed and her seed;
He shall bruise your head,
And you shall bruise His heel.

From the earliest scriptures the promise is there that one day a child would be born of a woman and crucially of her seed rather than a man's seed, and that child would have absolute authority and power to crush evil in this world, bruising the very head of the serpent.

Imagine Mary, a dispossessed person living under an oppressive regime, a woman living in a patriarchal society, hearing an angel tell her, "*The holy one to be born will be called the Son of God.*" Not only is God going to do this for all people, but he is also going to do it through *you*. Perhaps we might grasp her sense of wonder. The child born to her will be a "*holy one*" and will be recognized as "the Son of God." This is who Jesus is. Mary is pointing us unequivocally toward the uniqueness and divinity of Christ. Her recounting of Gabriel's prophecy is critical evidence for the nature and identity of Jesus as the Son of God. Theologians sometimes call this Christology. Mary is convinced. Her reply shows us that she believes that what she has heard will come to pass. Her fear is natural, and it is acknowledged, and her words echo through the pages of scripture and through the corridors of the ages, down to us today. She said to the angel: "*I am the Lord's servant. May your word to me be fulfilled.*" What outstanding faith!

As we walk through this Advent season and prepare our hearts to welcome and worship the Lord Jesus at Christmas, take some time to reflect on Mary's faith and say with her: "*I am your servant, Lord, may your word to me be fulfilled.*"

In this Advent season, perhaps we can draw encouragement from the simple but astonishing faith and obedience of a young woman. A young woman who understood theologically this magnificent intervention of God in human history and who said "yes," offering her own body willingly to this calling with these simple words: "*May your word to me be fulfilled.*"

Mary's involvement also points us to deep truth about how the incarnation was to unfold. Her question was: *How can this be?* The way God came in history matters as well as the fact of him coming. Some time ago, a teenager asked me if men and women are equal image bearers of God as Genesis 1:27 claims: "*So God created man* in His own *image; in the image of God He created him;* male and female He created them." Why did God come as a man? As we have seen, Genesis 3:15 contains a messianic promise given to Eve, promising that her seed will crush Satan and evil. God will come as a man in history and will be a woman's offspring. Through Mary's womb, God comes into the world as a man, but he is born of a woman. Jesus is born as a man, the Son of God in human history—but he is born of a woman. Both male and female play a unique and significant role in the incarnation of God.

Mary's response to the word of the Lord through Gabriel: "*May your word to me be fulfilled*" is preceded by the angel's promise: "*No word from God will ever fail.*"

PRAYER

We beseech thee, O Lord, pour thy grace into our
hearts; that, as we have known the incarnation of
thy Son Jesus Christ by the message of an angel, so
by his cross and passion we may be brought unto
the glory of his resurrection; through the same
Jesus Christ our Lord. Amen.

The Church of England Book of Common Prayer

Adam and Eve, Massolino, 1425, in the Cappella Brancacci, Florence, Italy.

This picture is a fresco on the wall of the Brancacci Chapel in Florence, Italy. It depicts Adam and Eve in the garden of Eden interacting with the Serpent. Eve's foot is on the base of the serpent's tail, and this speaks of the promise given to her by God that one day her seed would bruise the serpent. Mary is the daughter of Eve, through whom this Messianic promise is fulfilled. Her seed, through a virgin conception, is Jesus, and he will defeat evil through his incarnation, life, crucifixion, and resurrection. Massolino's painting humanizes the serpent, giving it a head that is capable of speech and expression, and the painting captures the very moment, where fruit in hand, both Adam and Eve are about to experience sin within their very bodies and souls. The moment of despair after this is depicted on the opposite wall in this chapel, with a mortified Eve. The "seed" of promise, Mary's son, will not only defeat evil, but he will also minister to those devastated in its wake.

Even Elizabeth your relative is going to have a child in her old age, and she who was said to be unable to conceive is in her sixth month. For no word from God will ever fail.…At that time Mary got ready and hurried to a town in the hill country of Judea, where she entered Zechariah's home and greeted Elizabeth. When Elizabeth heard Mary's greeting, the baby leaped in her womb, and Elizabeth was filled with the Holy Spirit. In a loud voice she exclaimed: "Blessed are you among women, and blessed is the child you will bear! But why am I so favored, that the mother of my Lord should come to me? As soon as the sound of your greeting reached my ears, the baby in my womb leaped for joy. Blessed is she who has believed that the Lord would fulfill his promises to her!"

Luke 1:36–45

In this Advent season, it is meaningful to take time to stop, reflect, and actively prepare our hearts for the coming of the Lord Jesus into this world. Mary's testimony gives us a unique and fresh perspective, given her unmistakable viewpoint on the central events around the birth of Jesus Christ. Today's scripture passage gives us insight into how Mary understood what was happening.

In the last two days, we have reflected on the interaction

between the Angel Gabriel and Mary following his announcement to her that she was going to give birth to a son unlike any person who has ever lived—*"the holy one to be born will be called the Son of God."* And today we consider what happened at the end of that encounter with Gabriel. Mary is told that Elizabeth, her relative, is going to have a child in her old age, and that *"she who was said to be unable to conceive is now in her sixth month of pregnancy. For no word from God will ever fail."*

Mary is going to give birth to a child, who will be Immanuel, God with us, who will be the Son of the Most High, and he will rule forever. The enormity of this truth is underscored by signs of confirmation to her. She, a virgin, will become pregnant by the power of the Holy Spirit, but there will also be a further sign. This is that her aged relative Elizabeth, who had been barren for years and years, is now also pregnant. In fact, Mary is told that Elizabeth is already in her sixth month at this point. As human beings, sometimes we need reassurance, we need signs and affirmations that we are headed in the right direction. We need to know at a deep level that we are on the right track. Mary is given her own virgin conception and the miraculous pregnancy of her aged, childless relative Elizabeth, as two tangible signs, so that she can know for certain that this really is God at work and it is not just her mind playing tricks on her.

Pregnancy is an extraordinary thing. Women all over the world will find their lives utterly changed and altered by pregnancy. And Elizabeth experienced exactly that. Her husband was a priest named Zechariah. He was a high-profile person, and so their barrenness as a couple was a cause of extraordinary shame for them, and a very public shame since childlessness was experienced as a deadly social and spiritual stigma. For Elizabeth, bearing a child would not have been a private experience. This birth was something that would be a miracle in the open and undeniably on the public record.

As a female relative, it would have been natural and even expected that Mary would go to visit Elizabeth at some point to congratulate her in her joy. But as Mary walks into Elizabeth's house, something extraordinary happens. At this point it is important to note there is no indication from the text that Mary had been in touch with Elizabeth, or that she had told her about the angel or that she had even told her she was in the early stages of pregnancy herself. As far as Elizabeth knew, her virgin, younger teenage relative was coming to her house to visit her. But as Mary walked into the house, the scriptures say that Elizabeth's child leaped within her.

I experienced a twin pregnancy, and so I felt a lot of pushing and shoving once the babies started kicking. But a baby absolutely leaping is something that would be very notable to a pregnant mother. Elizabeth at that moment of the baby leaping is filled with the Holy Spirit. "*When Elizabeth heard Mary's greeting, the baby leaped in her womb, and Elizabeth was filled with the Holy Spirit.*" The text says she was filled with the Holy Spirit and began to speak in a *loud* voice. She exclaimed an amazing blessing over Mary's life and the life she was carrying.

In that blessing, Elizabeth recognizes a profound spiritual truth about Jesus. She says, "*Who am I, that the mother of my*

Lord would come to my house?" Elizabeth is an older woman, a woman with more status than the younger woman, a woman who is in the midst of a public miracle herself that undoes decades of shame that she has lived under. Her mindset would have naturally been to celebrate her own miracle. She had no reason whatsoever to believe that an unmarried teenage relative coming into her house was pregnant. Let alone to honor the unborn child as her "Lord."

Her blessing exclaimed in a loud voice for all to hear says, not only do I see by the power of the Holy Spirit that you're carrying a child, but I am calling your unborn child *my Lord.* This is an electrifying theological revelation given by the power of the Holy Spirit to Elizabeth, the older woman, and spoken over Mary, the younger woman. Mary's unborn son is the Lord! What a confirming and encouraging word for Mary. The gift of prophecy, given to Elizabeth in the midst of her own life-changing miracle, points us toward the Lord Jesus and the magnitude of what it means that God took on human flesh in Jesus. That the Son of God was to be born of a woman.

Mary voices this to Luke so that we can hear it, which really matters. She needed those confirmations if she was going to be the primary witness to the incarnation of God. God made it so that along the way, these theological, historical, and miraculous revelations and signs are given to her so that she can believe and so that she can trust.

As we reflect on this today in our own Advent journeys, as we look toward celebrating the coming of the Lord Jesus at his birth and what that meant, from Mary's theological perspective, perhaps we can take a moment and wonder at the truth that a baby inside an older woman could recognize the coming of God in the womb of a younger woman.

PRAYER

Mighty God, by His grace, Elizabeth rejoiced with
Mary and greeted her as the mother of the Lord.
Look with favor on your lowly servants, that with
Mary, we may magnify your holy name and rejoice
to her claim her son, our Saviour, who is alive and
reigns with you in the unity of the Holy Spirit.
One God now and forever, Amen.

The Church of England Book of Common Prayer

The Visitation, Mariotto Albertinelli (Florence, 1474–1515),
Uffizi Gallery, Florence, Italy.

This painting of Mary and Elizabeth is contextualized in an architectural frame mirroring the church it was painted in. This places the theme of the image into the contemporary experience of the worshippers. It was originally placed in the Oratorio di San Michele Vecchio in Florence, Italy, for the altar and can now be seen in the Uffizi gallery. The main image places this story within three other narrative panels—the *Annunciation*, the *Nativity*, and the *Presentation in the Temple*—and is called a Predella. The greeting of Elizabeth and Mary belies a tenderness between the two women who are both simply dressed. The right hand is clasped beneath as the left hand is rested on a shoulder expressing warmth, fellowship, and compassion between an older and a younger woman. Both women are expecting babies, and both are caught up in a solidarity of providence. Albertinelli was the son of a goldsmith, yet he favored a style of painting that emphasized the humanity and earthy connection between his subjects and his audience. Much of his time as an artist was spent in close friendship with Fra Bartolomeo, with whom he set up a studio together where they split all profits and liabilities, and like Carravaggio they pursued a style that drew out intimacy rather than grandeur.

Blessed are you among women, and blessed is the child you will bear! But why am I so favored among women that the mother of my Lord should come to me? As soon as the sound of your greeting reached my ears, the baby in my womb leaped for joy. Blessed is she who has believed that the Lord would fulfil his promises to her!

Luke 1:43–45

Blessing and believing belong together in the scriptures. In the opening chapter of Luke's gospel, a contrast is drawn between Zechariah, the respected priest who had access to the temple and was chosen to burn incense on the altar, and his wife, Elizabeth. While Zechariah stood by the altar in the temple, a place of holiness and divine presence, he had not believed the Angel Gabriel when he appeared to him and promised him that his elderly wife Elizabeth would bear a child who would be "*a joy and delight to you, and many will rejoice because of his birth*" (Luke 1:14). Zechariah's failure to believe the direct words of prophecy about the arrival of John the Baptist resulted in him becoming mute until the day the child would be born.

It is in this context of her husband's silence that Elizabeth proclaims in a loud voice: "*Blessed are you among women and blessed is the child you will bear!*" As a blessed woman herself, on her way out of the shame and disappointment of barrenness, Elizabeth uses her voice and she proclaims her blessing with confidence. Elizabeth is carrying a child about whom the Angel Gabriel has prophesied, *"He will go on before the Lord, in the spirit and power of Elijah to turn the hearts of the parents to their children and the disobedient to the wisdom of the righteous—to make ready a people prepared for the Lord"* (Luke 1:17). But she sees that the child Mary is carrying is greater, and like John the Baptist will go ahead of Jesus, Elizabeth goes ahead of Mary, proclaiming the way of the Lord.

Elizabeth's choice of words emphasizes this: "*blessed* are you among women and *blessed* is the child"; the Greek word used twice here is *eulogemenos*, and it means to praise or *speak well*. The child Mary is carrying is praiseworthy, and Mary's role as mother speaks of that praise, which is ultimately God's. It is the fruit of Mary's womb that is worthy of praise, and her life speaks well among women as she believes, exercises faith, and walks in obedience to her calling.

Elizabeth, even as she has grasped the marvel of her own miracle, recognizes that something even more extraordinary and exceptional has happened to Mary, and she utters this phrase, "the mother of my Lord." The Eastern Church, the early church, called Mary *theotokos*, meaning "the Mother of God." It is a title that reflects upon what the incarnation means. The wonder of God in flesh entails the truth that Jesus was a human being, God was born in human history, and he had a mother.

Elizabeth goes on to use her voice to connect blessing and believing. In contrast to Elizabeth's husband, the one with priestly status, position, power, and opportunity, Mary has believed that the promise spoken to her is true. And as a consequence she is "blessed." The Greek word used here is *makaria*, meaning "happy."

Mary is presented by Elizabeth as a model for us as readers of the gospel—we should not be like Zechariah who didn't believe the promises he was given; we can hear the word and see the promises of God; we can encounter Jesus ourselves—and as we believe what is true, we too will be "blessed"—happy and fulfilled. Blessing and believing belong together. And it is no mistake that the weak, the powerless, the disregarded, the disempowered, the women, are able to see and trust. Mary's and Elizabeth's two voices are the chorus of witness. The representative of religious power has been silenced for a while, and the two eyewitnesses to the incarnation are humble women who have believed something true. This in itself is a cause for wonder, and it reminds us that when it comes to Jesus, outsiders are included, the humble are lifted up, and women have a voice. Happiness and fulfillment are to be found in believing the truth.

By contrast there is sorrow, frustration, anxiety, and disappointment when we trust in a story or person that turns out to be a deception. I have experienced that through being scammed online—thinking I was buying something only to have the seller disappear once the money had been transferred. I have experienced being lied to and deceived by people in authority seeking to prop up an institution; this often took the form of failing to correct errors or falsehoods that had been communicated confidently but turned out to be untrue. Such experiences leave us with a bitter taste in the mouth and make us wary of trusting again.

But Elizabeth's statement about Mary, *"Blessed is she who has believed that what the Lord has said to her will be fulfilled,"* reminds us that there is great blessing and happiness in believing the truth—and there is blessing in trusting that God's promises will be fulfilled. Ultimately that can only happen through the Lord Jesus, and Mary knew that. She understood that the son she would bear would be the one we all need to put our faith and trust in.

Blessing is to be found for any of us who believe that what the Lord has said will be fulfilled.

PRAYER

Almighty God, and most merciful Father,
we humbly submit ourselves, and fall down before
your Majesty, asking you from the bottom of our
hearts, that this seed of your Word now sown
among us, may take such deep root, that neither
the burning heat of persecution cause it to wither,
nor the thorny cares of this life choke it. But that, as
seed sown in good ground, it may bring forth thirty,
sixty, or a hundredfold, as your heavenly
wisdom has appointed. Amen.

Middelburg Liturgy

Illustration from Horarium Omnium Sanctorum, *The Book of Hours*,
Lambeth Palace Library, London.

This illuminated manuscript page is another one taken from the devotional book used for Christian prayer and worship, titled *The Book of Hours*, which could be used by religious communities, such as monks or nuns, or in the private chapels of wealthier landowners. The process of making the vellum for each page was expensive and difficult, meaning great care was taken when applying the words, decorations, illuminations, and figurative elements. Each page was created from animal skin that was stretched, cleaned, and smoothed successive times until it could take the ink and gilding. Here the painting style is quite naturalistic and shows the backdrop of contemporary medieval landscape and castles, with a young Mary painted in blue and the older Elizabeth in red. Paintings on a whole page, or within the calligraphy, gave the Flemish (Dutch-Belgian) artists and scriptwriters a chance to bring out styles, but also to bring emphasis. The two women are expressively drawn, reminding us that ordinary people are caught up in the purposes and plans of God.

And Mary said…

Luke 1:46

Today we focus on this small and seemingly insignificant phrase, *"and Mary said."* Luke has been careful to include Mary's detailed account of her experiences and observations in his gospel, and this approach makes this particular part of the Bible unique in literary and historical terms. Women's voices in history are rarely heard. Yet here we have Mary's eyewitness testimony included in a broader account, alongside her actual words. Mary's voice matters.

The words of the Magnificat that follow form the longest speech of any woman in the New Testament, and it is clear from the format that Mary's words are following long-established patterns of prophecy and praise that are known in the Old Testament. The teenage Mary is filled with the Holy Spirit, and the words of the Magnificat pour out of her. Later on, Luke—who is also the author of the book of Acts—notes that Mary is present at Pentecost, when the flames of the Holy Spirit descended, as *"Mary the mother of Jesus"* was named among the disciples and women who had gathered in the upper room (Acts 1:14) to pray.

John in his gospel identifies Jesus's mother as being with

her son during his ministry a number of times—and on each occasion he presents her in a positive light. The first instance is at the wedding at Cana where Mary launches her son's ministry by instigating his miracle of transforming water into wine (John 2:1–11), and her speech is recorded when she says to the servants, *"Do whatever he tells you."*

A woman could speak, and her words are recorded for us as meaningful, insightful, and weighty in the scriptures. It seems to me that many Christians gloss over the significance of this. But there are not many other ancient texts from the era—either religious or historical—that value the voices of women enough to record them.

"And Mary said…"

There are important parallels that can be made between Mary and Abraham. For example, Mary received a divine annunciation regarding her miraculously conceived firstborn son—just as Abraham met an angel who prophesied that he and Sarah would have Isaac. In John's gospel, Mary's son carried the wood for his own sacrifice on his back up the mountain—just as Isaac carried the wood up Mount Moriah. Mary stood on top of Golgotha's hill at her son's place of crucifixion and sacrifice—just as Abraham stood on top of Mount Moriah. In fact, it is the same mountain. Some scholars argue that the gospel authors saw Mary as "the New Abraham," and so a Judean woman could be both a mother and a leader who had theological symbolic significance in her own person but could also share her insights with the world.

"And Mary said…"

The very fact of the Magnificat tells us what it was morally possible for a woman to do with her words. Mary's use of her voice in the gift of prophecy and ethical teaching and praise that flows forth resonates strongly with images of her captured by the early church. Her arms and eyes are raised in benediction in the earliest depictions; it is only later after the 1500s that images of Mary tend to depict her with her eyes cast down and her hands withdrawn in a posture of passivity.

One of the most striking phenomena about the early church that was noted at the time was that women appear to have been exceptionally involved in the spread of the faith. Among the house churches named in the New Testament, many are associated with the name of the women who helped lead them: Chloe, Nympha, Apphia, Priscilla, Lydia, and Mary the mother of Mark. In Romans 16, the work of several women is mentioned and affirmed—Phoebe, Prisca, Mary, Junia, Tryphaena, Tryphosa, Rufus's mother, Julia, and Nereus's sister.

Roman and Greek writers outside the Christian faith also indicated that its women leaders were publicly visible. For example, the first Roman to write about "Christians" was Pliny the Younger, who was the governor of Bithynia and Pontus. Around the year 113, Pliny questioned several of Jesus's followers as part of his investigations for the emperor about Christianity—and when he needed to find out more details, he interrogated two women whom he called *ministrae*, or ministers (Pliny the Younger, *Epistle*, 10.96).

"And Mary said…"

Here at the beginning of Luke's gospel, Mary is opening a

new chapter, an era that will in part fulfill Joel's prophecy from the Old Testament: *"Even on my servants, both men and women, I will pour out my Spirit in those days"* (Joel 2:29). The gospel of Jesus Christ ushers in this era. We do not need to be a particular race, class, or biological sex to be included in the promise. At Pentecost, Peter preached from this very passage, going on to affirm that *"the promise is for you and your children and for all who are far off—for all whom the Lord our God will call"* (Acts 2:39).

If you have felt discarded, excluded, or in some way hindered from fully receiving the promises of God and the fullness of the Holy Spirit, perhaps today you might see that the wonder of the gospel includes you.

PRAYER

I bind myself today:
To the power of God to guide me.
To the might of God to uphold me.
To the wisdom of God to teach me.
The eye of God to watch over me.
The ear of God to hear me.
The word of God to speak to me.
The way of God to lie before me.
The host of God to defend me. Amen.

St. Patrick

Illustration from Horarium Omnium Sanctorum, *The Book of Hours*,
Lambeth Palace Library, London.

This close-up on the illustrated manuscript *The Book of Hours* is from the early fifteenth century. The artist brings together the Annunciation (the moment Gabriel comes to Mary) with the Magnificat—the first word in Latin for her prophetic song "my soul magnifies the Lord." Mary is shown as an important prophet of the New Testament, a teacher and writer of scripture. The specific words of Gabriel unfurl like a scroll, and Mary, responding to this word, sits down and sees what she hears as scripture in a book that she is holding. We can imagine monks, nuns, theologians, and worshippers, then holding this *Book of Hours*, singing the text of the Magnificat, following on from what the image portrays.

And Mary said: "My soul magnifies the Lord, and My spirit rejoices in God my Savior."

Luke 1:46–47

In today's scripture, Mary begins with the words *"my soul."* Often in church history or art, Mary has been viewed as an empty vessel, a blank slate, whose sole purpose is birthing. But here her personhood is more broadly affirmed. Mary's soul magnifies the Lord. She is first and foremost a worshipper. Her identity is not primarily about her ministry role, significant as that is in salvation history. Her identity is not even determined by the biological potential of her body. Mary is a soul—a person. And her personhood is expressive—she is a woman whose very breath speaks of the greatness of God. She magnifies or exalts the Lord—declaring that God is great.

Sometimes in the Christian life we can become performative. We behave as if our primary sense of why we are here on this earth is to do certain things. Perhaps our ministry output or our parental status takes over our entire thinking and being. I remember in the early stages of motherhood how daunting and overwhelming it felt to have twin babies completely dependent on me. It felt as if people no longer interacted with me as someone who had her own thoughts, feelings, insights, or preferences. In many settings I was the mother of twins, and nothing more. Entire conversations were conducted with a person looking at the babies and not even catching my eye. I even found that my own overwhelming love for my babies and the physical demands of caring for them impacted my sense of self. My own needs seemed so unimportant. Here we encounter Mary as a person, expressing her dignity and humanity by worshipping God with her inmost being. She is not subsumed into the role of mother—she is able to express the worship of her soul to her creator, and to reflect theologically upon what has happened at the incarnation.

This opening phrase of the Magnificat, *"My soul magnifies,"* signals to us that Mary knew the Old Testament. Her praise is infused with the language of scripture; it is connected to the history and worship of God's people in the past. Mary's opening to the Magnificat clearly and intentionally echoes Hannah's song of praise that she sang when she had given birth to a longed-for son named Samuel after a time of prolonged infertility. Hannah began, *"My heart rejoices in the Lord"* (1 Samuel 2:1). Mary, by echoing these words, identifies with Hannah, connecting her own story with the history, prophecy, and Messianic hope of the Old Testament. Mary and Hannah are both mothers rejoicing over the conception or birth of an unexpected but God-given child. Hannah's praise flows from the end of her barrenness, while Mary's flows from her amazement at the miracle of the virgin conceiving the Son of God. The stories remind us of each other, reassuring us that God is at work in human history and that he can be trusted. This is important because although the songs begin with joy, both women would come to know the sorrow of being called to give up their sons.

As Mary now begins to speak, taking a lead from her foremother Hannah, praise pours forth from her. And as she carries the very savior of the world in her womb, she speaks of her spirit rejoicing in God *her* savior. This theologically rich phrase of praise weaves together the promises of Gabriel that the child should be given the name Jesus, which means to deliver, rescue, or save, and the promise that he would be the "*son of the Most High*." These truths join with the inspired words of Elizabeth, that Mary is carrying "*My Lord*" in her womb. As Mary's Spirit rejoices in God her savior, the savior of the world is within her womb. This is the moment that the entire history of the world had been leading up to. The New Testament later describes this moment in this way: "*But when the set time had fully come, God sent his Son, born of a woman, born under the law to redeem those under the law that we might receive adoption to sonship*" (Galatians 4:4–5). God in Christ is the savior who would redeem us and enable us to become children of God.

This is a simple and embodied truth. Carrying a child to term is an overwhelming physical experience. My first experience of this was my twin pregnancy. Every movement was a wonder as limbs and elbows pushed and prodded. I remember at one scan appointment seeing one of the babies stretch out and the other immediately retaliated with his elbow—giving his brother a big shove. Mary knew what it was to carry a child who was destined to be the savior of the world. But he nonetheless grew and developed and moved within her, a real pregnancy with all of the physicality that entails.

Mary rejoices in her song in *"God my Savior."* She is singing to God and she is singing about her son. She knows that her unborn son is already the one who will be the savior of the world. He is already there inside her womb as a baby, growing and forming. Their identities are not mingled or confused. It seems clear that there is a distinction of persons here; Jesus is not an extension of Mary's body; he is already a separate individual. And Mary is a person who is capable of praise and who is able to recognize her own need of a savior outside of herself. But that savior, the Son of God, is now growing and developing within her. This is demonstrably the case since Elizabeth and her unborn son were able to acknowledge and recognize him. And now Mary does the same, speaking out her words of worship and honor.

No wonder praise flows from her lips. This is a moment for adoration, wonder, and glory.

PRAYER

And now we give you thanks, because
by the power of the Holy Spirit,
Jesus took our nature upon him and was born
of the Virgin Mary, his mother, that being
himself without sin, he might make us
clean from all sin. Amen.

The Church of England Book of Common Prayer

Madonna and Child, Duccio di Buoninsegna (1290–1300),
Metropolitan Museum, New York.

The Italian painter Duccio di Buoninsegna created this painting in the late 1200s. He was one of a group of artists who drew on the icon traditions of the East and blended this style with an earthier and more rounded approach to painting that emphasized everyday life. Here Mary is framed in gold to draw our attention to her place in the sacred story. Her child touches her face, pushing back her hair and veil and peering intently into her eyes, showing us by contrast her everyday humanity. The picture is both sacred and intimate—which is further underlined by the burn marks on the frame reminding us of hundreds of years of flickering candlelight, from candles held too close. We the observers are invited closer in—to see the truth of the incarnation—humanity and divinity held together.

He has been mindful of the humble state of his servant. From now on all generations will call me blessed.

Luke 1:48

Mary muses here that God "has been mindful" of her—this is resonant of the Psalmist's words in the Old Testament: "*What is man that you are mindful of him,* **the son of man that you care for him?** *You made him a little lower than the heavenly beings and crowned him with glory and honor*" (Psalm 8:4–5). By referencing this Psalm, Mary is locating her experience within the arc of salvation history. She is praising God that she, a mere mortal, is "crowned with glory and honor" by virtue of her status as a human being at all, since God is mindful of us. But *mindful* might also be translated with a further meaning as "looked with favor," and in this sense the phrase goes beyond the application of Psalm 8 to all human beings pointing us toward the particular divine favor that Mary has experienced.

This sense of God's favor draws out the unique calling that Mary has received to be the Mother of Christ and acknowledges the assignment as a blessing. Although it must have felt overwhelming, in her heart Mary has counted this as favor.

Perhaps she has remembered the prophecy of Isaiah that one day a virgin would conceive a child. *"Behold, a virgin shall conceive and bear a son, and shall name him Emmanuel"* (Isaiah 7:14)—that is, "God with us." And in his eternal wisdom Mary was to be that one.

Mary is deeply aware that even as the God of the universe is mindful of her—what he would find when he specifically had her in mind would be "the humble state of his servant." The description she used of herself could be a bond slave, the lowest class of servant girl in the Roman Empire. This sense of abject humility is true to her status in the global power dynamics of her age. Mary was female, she was young, she was part of a despised and occupied nation, she had no formal education, and she was poor. Yet in this verse, she says GOD is mindful of her humble class, biological sex, race, and political agency. He is mindful of all of that. But Mary's humble state is not an inconvenience to God—it matters, it is a vital part of the story, because her humility speaks of the gospel—it points to the kind of savior Jesus is. The gospels go on to emphasize at every turn that the humble are lifted up, the repentant find mercy, the weak and abused are welcomed, and the hungry are filled with good things. Because that is the way of Jesus. In fact, Mary's words serve as a reminder along with the rest of the Bible that God is not partial to the rich, the powerful, or the proud. The things that in our world most often serve as idols or substitutes for God—namely, money, power, pride, and prestige—do not qualify us for God's favor.

In fact, the contrast of Mary's humble origins, with the magnitude of the blessing of her calling to be the mother of the Son of God, demonstrates that the hand of God is at work in blessing her so that *"From now on all generations will call me blessed."*

All generations include all races, all families and people of all ages and time periods. *"All generations"* is a big claim—Mary is saying that the Salvation of God through the child she will bear will not just be a blessing for a limited or immediate time period. Jesus is not going to be born to only deliver people of Mary's generation from the spiritual and political captivity they are experiencing. Mary has understood that the level of blessing she is experiencing—the magnitude of God being born as a baby—will cause all generations to take note. The salvation and blessing that Jesus will bring in history will transcend time—operating backward and forward. People in the Old Testament looked forward to the coming Messiah through the sacrificial system and the law, and received the benefits of Christ by faith even though he was as yet unseen. Furthermore, everyone who lived at the time of Christ and after his resurrection could receive salvation through Jesus regardless of status, ethnicity, biological sex, age, or class.

It is because of who Jesus is that all generations will call Mary blessed. This is not a comment on her own status, which she has already noted makes her a bondslave. The unlikelihood of a girl from Nazareth being called anything by anyone should not be lost on us. Mary was a peasant girl from a neighborhood where her kin were carpenters in Nazareth, a village so insignificant that it is not mentioned in the Old Testament, in the writings of the historian Josephus (c. 37–100), or in the Jewish Talmud. *"Can anything good come from Nazareth?"* asked Nathanael (John 1:46, NLT). Her angelic encounter with the Angel Gabriel took place in an unknown, ordinary house, not in the temple.

Yet Elizabeth, the wife of the priest Zechariah—who served in the Temple in Jerusalem—has just greeted her as the mother of my Lord, and from now on all generations will know of this blessing. That God has come to this world—that God would be born of a woman. And that Jesus would make Mary happy, complete, fulfilled, and blessed.

As I reflect on this today, I think of ours and future generations—will we call Mary blessed? Will we hear of the coming of the Lord Jesus? Will we have the opportunity to hear the truest of true stories: that the God who created this universe entered into it as a human being and was born of a woman? That he would go on to claim to be the only true source of eternal life, and peace for human beings: *"I am the bread of life; whoever comes to me will never go hungry, and whoever believes in me will never be thirsty"* (John 6:35)?

Let the wonder of that sink in.

And take heart in this Advent season that you and I are not alone in reflecting upon how blessed Mary was to play this role in the incarnation of God. All around the world millions of people are part of the fulfillment of her words.

"From now on all generations will call me blessed."

PRAYER

God our redeemer,
who prepared the Blessed Virgin Mary
to be the mother of your Son:
grant that, as she looked for his coming as our
saviour,
so we may be ready to greet him
when he comes again as our judge;
who is alive and reigns with you,
in the unity of the Holy Spirit,
one God, now and for ever. Amen.

The Church of England Book of Common Prayer

Illustration, Beatus Vir from Vaux Psalter manuscript (early 1300s),
Lambeth Palace Library.

This is an illustrated manuscript called the Vaux Psalter. It is illustrating Psalm 1, and begins in Latin *Beatus Vir*, meaning "blessed is the man." The book is housed in the Lambeth Palace Library and was thought to have been created between 1310 and 1320 for an educated woman from York, in the North of England. It is a book of Psalms and scriptures designed to be sung devotionally at home or in a chapel. The connection between the original owner of the book, a young woman from the Vaux family, and Mary, a young woman caught up in song and praise, is beautifully drawn out. Almost the entire page is taken up with the letter "B"—for Beatus...blessed. The letter is filled with pictures of prophets and the many generations before Christ who look forward to his birth, death, and Resurrection. The illustrator places the word *blessed* within a family tree, linking the idea of "generations" to the coming of Christ and to the "tree planted by streams of water" in Psalm 1. Mary is positioned in the center of it all, depicted at the crucifixion where Jesus dies on a tree.

For the Mighty One has done great things for me.

Luke 1:49

Mary reminds us in this sentence that God is "*The Mighty One*" and that "*he has done great things for me.*" The great theological and philosophical truth that God is transcendent and that he is MIGHTY is coupled together with "*he has done great things for me.*" That same almighty and all-powerful God is also personal since he has looked upon me—"*he has done great things for me.*" Mary, the teenage girl from Nazareth, captures something deeply profound in this sentence about the transcendence and immanence of God. She proclaims that God is the Mighty One, sovereign over all—over creation, over the material world, over time and space, over reason and emotion, over history, over rulers and systems—AND he has done something beautiful for me.

This is the first attribute of God that Mary explores and speaks of in the Magnificat—God's might and power. He is the mighty God, *ho dunatos* in Greek. Mary's God was God Almighty, the Creator of the ends of the earth. There is no one mightier than her God. He alone is able, and with God nothing is impossible. It is clear again that Mary knew the

Old Testament scriptures, and how much they shape her song. God himself spoke of this aspect of his character to Abraham in Genesis 17:1 where he is revealed as *El Shaddai*. The Lord Almighty. God Almighty is a name for God given forty-eight times in the Old Testament.

I remember as a teenager a particular experience of the power of God. It was the summer of 1991. The Berlin Wall had fallen in November 1989 and Eastern Europe was opening up. My grandparents had escaped from Soviet occupation, and none of us in the family had been able to go behind the iron curtain as a consequence. I now had the opportunity to join a mission trip to the Czech Republic, and we were in Prague sharing the gospel of Jesus through performing arts. At one point in Wenceslas Square after a large crowd of over one thousand had gathered, one of the leaders turned to me and invited me to speak. I had no real training and I felt completely overwhelmed. But the power of God carried me, and people listened and responded to the message. That was the first time I ever preached. At the end I knew it was God who gave me the ability to preach. This was a memorable experience of "*the Mighty One has done great things for me.*"

God as Almighty is called El Shaddai in the Old Testament scriptures, and his power and might are contrasted with the idols of the nations who in Hebrew are called *sheddim*. They are dependent on their worshippers since those idols are created by humans, either by our minds or by our hands. *Sheddim* means they are not self-sustaining. But God Almighty, El Shaddai, is by contrast all sufficient—he is not in need of therapy from humanity and he is not a figment of our minds or something made for our convenience. He is Almighty and entirely sovereign over all things visible or invisible, powers, ages, objects, or systems. But Shaddai also carries the root word for "of the bosom of the mother"; El Shaddai is an extraordinarily intimate kind of Almightyness. Just as we are nursed and fed the milk of our human mothers, so we need to be sustained and nurtured by the one who is utterly Almighty. In the storms of life he is mighty and powerful, but he also is tender and nurturing as a mother with a baby. Mary speaks of God as Almighty and *all* powerful, and this is resonant with the Lord Almighty, El Shaddai.

The power and majesty of Almighty God will be revealed through Christ. In Matthew 19:26 Jesus Christ says, "*With man this is impossible, but with God all things are possible.*" The apostle Paul recognized this too and wrote in Ephesians 3:20, "*Now to him who is able to do immeasurably more than all we ask or imagine.*" Mary adds her voice to these: "*for the Mighty One has done great things for me.*"

Here, Mary holds together these two theological thoughts. God is the Mighty one who is transcendent and holy and glorious and magnificent beyond our wildest imaginations. He is the source of philosophical and theological, metaphysical truth and reality, and he is the creator of material creation. He is the powerful and mighty Lord of all. And it is *he* who has done great things *for me.*

She brings together this transcendent, marvelous, wonderful God with the one who actually interacts with you and me in space and time in history. She brings together the transcendence and the immanence of God. Isn't that exactly what we see in the incarnation? We see the transcendent Creator God, becoming immanent, drawing close, taking on human flesh coming to dwell among us. Mary grasps this tenderness of God, and like a psalmist, or a prophet of old, she extols God with these wonderful theological truths: *"My soul glorifies and magnifies the Lord—the Mighty One has done great things for me."*

Perhaps like Mary today we might think about and give thanks for the specific and wonderful things the Lord the Mighty One has done for us in our lives. But before we jump to making lists of things he has done, for which we are thankful, dwell for a moment on the tenderness of Almighty God, his love for you personally and his desire to interact with you, to carry and strengthen you even in times of great turmoil and difficulty.

PRAYER

O Lord, who hast mercy upon all,
take away from me my sins,
and mercifully kindle in me
the fire of thy Holy Spirit.
Take away from me the heart of stone,
and give me a heart of flesh,
a heart to love and adore Thee,
a heart to delight in Thee,
to follow and enjoy Thee,
for Christ's sake, Amen.

St. Ambrose of Milan

Mary, Charlie Mackesy, private collection, London, 2022.

Charlie Mackesy is a British artist, illustrator, and author of *New York Times* bestseller *The Boy, the Mole, the Fox and the Horse*. His paintings of the Prodigal Son feature in churches and galleries in London. In this painting from his private collection, he captures Mary as a young woman in charcoal. Mackesy depicts Mary's womanhood with a rare combination of depth and approachability. This piece is not available for public view, underscoring Mary as personal, real, and human. Mary's vulnerability and strength draw us in with admiration, without placing her on an unattainable pedestal. Charcoal, which is made from burned wood, hints at the suffering that is to come, and his use of contrasting light and dark adds drama and pathos to the image.

Holy is his name.

Luke 1:49

The cultural context of Mary's day was one that regarded women with suspicion, and as particularly vulnerable to disordered desire and moral weakness. Bearing this in mind, it is noteworthy that Mary is able to speak of the idea of God having "*done great things for me*," which we explored yesterday, alongside a declaration that he is Holy. God's holiness and his kindness are not in contradiction with each other.

In her declaration "*Holy is his name*," Mary exalts in the holiness of God. Knowing her own frailty, her lowly status, and her humble origins, Mary sees that God's holiness is something to rejoice in. And Mary's mention of God's "name" speaks of his essence, his character, his being. A name summed up the origin, personhood, and ethos of someone in the ancient world. By speaking of God's name, Mary points us to God as personal and trustworthy. God's holiness and his identity are closely intertwined for her.

God's holiness is often thought of as his otherness—his distance, his purity, or his separateness. Holiness is frequently characterized negatively by human beings so that to be holy is to be spotless or without sin. But here Mary speaks of God as holy in a more deeply biblical way. His holiness is something positive and holistic—it is his utter integrity. Wholeness within his own being, *"Holy is his name"*—characterizes God as profoundly truthful to his loving, perfect self.

We may well come across people in our lives who are not at peace with themselves. At the core of who they are is an internal conflict or a crushing sense of inferiority. This makes for danger, unhappiness, and disharmony. My father-in-law always used to say, "Never trust a person who is not easy in their own skin." Regardless of class, socioeconomic background, color, biological sex, or any other distinguishing feature, this was the most significant for him. He had noticed in his decades of life that a person who was in internal conflict was not a safe person to do business with. God's holiness is a profound integrity, coherence, peace, and unity within himself.

Mary reminds us that Jesus's incarnation points us toward God's holiness not exclusively as separateness or otherness or distance, but she points to holiness as wholeness, perfection, goodness, beauty, and truth. The most perfect human who ever lived, the most whole and good and true person, Jesus Christ, is able to perfectly demonstrate the love and goodness of God. Holy is his name.

Mary's connection of God's holiness with his *name* is also a reminder that this is an issue of God's essential identity being communicated to us. A name designates God as personal and knowable. The God of the Bible is not an abstract philosophical entity, a concept to be defended. He is the God who is there, the God who is knowable by us, the God who is revealed and named throughout the scriptures. He is the God who desires connection with us, and this is an aspect of his holiness.

In calling God holy, Mary is referring to something that is difficult for our finite minds to comprehend since God's holiness also encompasses his eternality—he is without beginning or end, and his moral character is ongoingly good and true. Holiness may also refer to his presence, knowledge, justice, exercise of power, and wisdom.

A name is given, bestowed, and considered. A name imparts meaning, value, identity, and significance. Your name was considered by your parents, and it was chosen specifically and especially for you. A name recognizes the humanity and dignity of a person. Which is why naming a baby feels like an awesome task. When I discovered I was expecting a baby, it wasn't until the first scan that I became clear that there were two babies inside. My husband leaped up and shouted, "Praise the Lord!" and the sonographer looked up, smiled, and quipped, "That is not usually the reaction of an expectant father when he hears there are twins." We decided not to find out the biological sex of the babies, which meant that we needed to come up with quite a lot of name possibilities in the different combinations.

A Godless culture loses the value of human life, and when the image of God slips away people quickly become reduced to biological matter, statistics, or just nameless commodities. The Nazis numbered and branded people in their camps, and the leaders of Apartheid in South Africa refused to call people by their given names, substituting easily pronounceable colonial names to children in schools. Names personalize and dignify. God gave Adam and Eve the task of naming the different creatures of his beautiful creation. A name bestows worth and value.

And so, Mary reflects that God is named, he is personal and dignified and knowable, and he is holy. He is entirely true to his character and perfect in all his ways in eternity, past, present, and future. He alone is worthy of our worship. And he can be trusted.

The book of Romans ends with a few words of praise that speak of the overwhelming beauty of the holiness of God.

Oh, the depth of the riches of the wisdom and knowledge
  of God!
How unsearchable his judgments,
and his paths beyond tracing out!
"Who has known the mind of the Lord?
Or who has been his counselor?"
"Who has ever given to God,
that God should repay them?"
For from him and through him and for him are all things.
To him be the glory forever! Amen. (Romans 11:33–36)

May we see something of the holiness of God today, and like Mary, may it cause us to worship Him in spirit and in truth.

PRAYER

Almighty God,
by whose grace alone we are accepted
and called to your service:
strengthen us by your Holy Spirit
and make us worthy of our calling;
through Jesus Christ our Lord. Amen.

The Church of England Book of Common Prayer

Giotto, Scrovegni Chapel, Padua, Italy, 1305.

Giotto was an artist who mastered the fresco style of paint onto plaster. He filled an entire chapel, floor to ceiling, with paintings in the Augustinian monastery in Padua, Italy, in 1305. It was declared a UNESCO world heritage site in 2021. Free from the strict artistic confines of the Byzantine style, which had developed from Eastern iconography, Giotto brings light and emotional depth and liveliness to the scene, known by many as the *Deposition*. This moment in which Mary, with others at the crucifixion, mourns the death of her son, is accompanied by an angelic host. It is a holy moment as she looks into the face of Jesus, whose integrity and calling have brought him to this sacrifice.

His mercy extends to those who fear him from generation to generation.

Luke 1:50

In Latin, mercy is *merced* and it means "price paid"; in Greek it is *eleos*, which means "mercy, pity, or compassion." To show mercy is to show compassion to those in distress, especially when it is in our power to punish or eviscerate. The psalmist says in the Old Testament, "*Have mercy upon me O God according to your unfailing love; according to your great compassion blot out my transgressions*" (Psalm 51:1). God's mercy is his compassion, and ultimately his forgiveness is extended to us who are transgressors. Here, Mary reminds us that God is a God who shows mercy to those who fear him.

During the Second World War a Dutch family living under Nazi occupation helped Jewish people to hide or to escape Holland. They themselves were captured, and two sisters—Corrie and Betsie ten Boom—were sent to the Ravensbrück concentration camp. Betsie died there. After the war, Corrie was speaking in a church and found herself face-to-face with one of the camp officials. He had come to hear her in the hope that she might offer him forgiveness. When he offered her his hand, she prayed, "Jesus, help me. I can lift my hand. I can do that much. You supply the feeling." She writes:

"And so woodenly, mechanically, I thrust my hand into the one stretched out to me. And as I did, an incredible thing took place. The current started in my shoulder, raced down my arm, sprang into our joined hands. And then this healing warmth seemed to flood my whole being, bringing tears to my eyes. 'I forgive you, brother!' I cried. 'With all my heart!' For a long moment we grasped each other's hands, the former guard and former prisoner. I had never known God's love so intensely as I did then."[1]

Mercy is a beautiful and unusual thing.

Given Mary's position as the mother of Jesus, the one through whom the savior of the world will be born, perhaps it is no surprise that she points us toward God's mercy. After all, that is why Jesus is coming into the world: to bring forgiveness to those who need it. To save us.

This hope for mercy has never been more relevant than it is for us today. In our day we are more likely to expect cancel culture than mercy. Cancel culture could be described as the impetus to punish a person whose ideas or behavior we disagree with by withdrawing support, ceasing communication with, and encouraging others to shun the transgressor. This may involve lobbying to get a person fired, or blacklisted from social occasions, membership of a community, or from speaking, publishing, or lecturing. Cancel culture involves exerting

---

1 https://www.guideposts.org/better-living/positive-living/guideposts
-classics-corrie-ten-boom-forgiveness.

social pressure and threatening ostracization or mass outrage if a person expresses unpopular or controversial opinions. Once canceled there is no hope for a person to receive public forgiveness and much less for redemption. Public floggings are back in the form of group shaming and boycotting, but it seems forgiveness is gone, an echo of a distant age. Accountability is everything; redemption is impossible.

Mary expressed her hope and belief in God's mercy that could extend to us through all generations. She is pointing us to the truth that faith that is shaped by the historic personality of Jesus Christ has something truly profound to offer us. The instinct in cancel culture that someone must pay and even die some kind of death for their transgression points beyond itself to an echo of the gospel story that has given meaning to millions around the world for over two thousand years. Jesus of Nazareth, as God incarnate, God in the flesh, willingly died by crucifixion at the hands of the Romans. His death is described in the New Testament as a ransom, an offering, and a sacrifice. He pays a price for the transgressions of the world. And that means forgiveness can be real. The mercy that Mary sang of is actually possible. The price we all intuitively sense must be paid was actually paid by Jesus.

Forgiveness has been rejected as a concept by the crusaders of cancel culture who see it as a weakness that denies the seriousness of wrongdoing. But Christian mercy and forgiveness does not say the thing that happened didn't hurt, it wasn't wrong, or it didn't matter. Forgiveness means that the incident did hurt, it was wrong, and it does matter—but there is power to forgive, because I trust that justice will ultimately be done. The transgression will be judged by a higher authority than me, or any of us, and if true repentance and ownership of our wrongdoing is offered to God, we can be forgiven in an ultimate sense—because someone HAS paid. God's mercy is possible because of Christ's sacrifice. Christian forgiveness underlines the seriousness of the hurt and evil that has occurred, since forgiving it requires the suffering and death of God.

Desmond Tutu wrote: "Forgiving is not forgetting; it's actually remembering—remembering and not using your right to hit back. It's a second chance for a new beginning. And the remembering part is particularly important. Especially if you don't want to repeat what happened."

The mercy and forgiveness that Mary speaks of lies in the realm of possibility not by denying the potency of the hurt or the seriousness of the action, but because a price has been paid for human wrongdoing in the death of God in history. And that means that there is power outside of ourselves to receive forgiveness and to give it.

The longing for mercy is an eternal reality—every generation needs it. And so this truth that Mary is extolling is not just true at an individual level; in Jesus, mercy will extend from generation to generation.

In this Advent time why not give thanks for God's mercy in your own life, which is only possible because of the coming of Jesus in history. And consider, Is there a person I need to extend forgiveness and mercy to in this season?

PRAYER

Disturb us, O Lord
when we are too well-pleased with ourselves
when our dreams have come true because
we dreamed too little,
because we sailed too close to the shore.
Disturb us, O Lord
when with the abundance of things we possess,
we have lost our thirst for the water of life
when, having fallen in love with time,
we have ceased to dream of eternity
and in our efforts to build a new earth,
we have allowed our vision of Heaven to grow dim.
Stir us, O Lord
to dare more boldly, to venture into wider seas
where storms show Thy mastery,
where losing sight of land, we shall find the stars.
In the name of Him who pushed back
the horizons of our hopes
and invited the brave to follow. Amen.

Desmond Tutu, adapted from an original prayer by Sir Francis Drake

Christ Nailed to the Cross, by Gerard David, the National Gallery, London.

This picture was originally painted in 1481 as the central part of three paintings (a triptych); the side panels are in Holland (*Pilate's Dispute with the High Priest* [left wing] and *The Holy Women and Saint John* [right wing], in the Koninklijk Museum voor Schone Kunsten Antwerpen). This section is housed at the National Gallery in London. Although Jesus was of Semitic ancestry, the artist pays meticulous attention to the taut sinews of Savior, as he is crucified, and paints the skin as almost translucent to bring attention to the veins and scratches. A small dog examines mortality in the shape of a skull and discarded bones, and a single blue robe is cast aside, alongside a soldier in a game of dice. Apart from the strong diagonal forces of this crucifixion, what makes this painting so striking is the way Jesus fixes his gaze on the viewer, as if to say in his pain, "I died for you." Jesus is the one through whom God extends mercy, even down through the generation, just as Mary prophesied. The painting imagines this mercy as extended to every observer.

He has performed mighty deeds with his arm.

Luke 1:51

Right in the middle of her hymn of praise, reverence, and adoration, Mary uses this phrase referring to God's arm: *"He has shown strength with His arm."* Mary gives us an image of God in human form, in which his arm is a symbol of his strength. This seems to be a reference to Numbers 11, and it shows us again that Mary was well versed in the Old Testament and that she was theologically astute. She is reminding us that the arm of the Lord is NOT too short to save. God showing strength in his arm is a reminder to us of the provision of God in the past, in the scriptures, and in our lives. Mary points us to a God who can be trusted and who will not fail his people.

One of the stranger chapters in the Bible is Numbers 11. It is an account of something that happened after the people of Israel had been delivered from slavery in Egypt. Moses was distraught because the multitude of people he had led out of Egypt in the exodus were now continually complaining to him. Day after day they were letting him know that they wanted to go back to Egypt, even if it meant returning to slavery, because they missed the food. They were fed up with the bread from heaven—the manna that God was supernaturally providing each.

The Israelites had grown sick and tired of the manna. The repetitiveness of the food became symptomatic of their desire to return to their old lives, and so after all of the turmoil and confrontation involved in standing up to Pharaoh, after the miracles of the parting of the Red Sea and the drinking water provided from a rock, after the long journeys being guided by a pillar of cloud by day and a pillar of fire by night, the people had had enough.

They couldn't take it anymore, and they said they wanted to go back to Egypt. They asked Moses, their leader, to take them back to the leadership of Pharaoh. Because at least under Pharaoh, even though they were slaves, they had a more varied diet—and specifically they had onions, garlic, and leeks to eat. The Old Testament says that Moses was so discouraged that he wanted to die. He said, *"Did I give birth to these people? Do I have to listen to this? They are crying in my tent, 'Give us meat to eat.'"* God responded to Moses, *"The Lord will give you meat…not for just one day, or two days, or five…but for a whole month, until it comes out of your nostrils and you loathe it"* (Numbers 11:19–20).

Now Moses was even more distressed and upset; he could not see how God might do this. He worried that all their herds would need to be killed to supply meat for a month for the number of people involved. He worried that the sea would be emptied of fish so as to feed them. And he says, *"This is even more than you can do."*

God answered with a question. He said to Moses, "*Is the Lord's arm too short?*"

Is God's arm too short to save? Is God going to fail? That is the question that precedes God providing quail birds to eat alongside the manna. God can provide food in a wilderness, daily, for thousands of people year in year out. That is the image that finds its way into this song: "*He has shown strength with His arm.*"

Mary believes that God is strong, consistent, faithful, and powerful to provide. She knows that God has provided for his people in the past, and this is the basis of her hope in him. God has displayed the strength in his arm through mighty deeds. Her words are defiant and powerful, anointed and prophetic.

And today we also need to remember that the arm of the Lord is not too short to save. "*He has shown strength in his arm*" reminds us of the provision of God in the past, in the scriptures, in our lives, and is a basis for hope and trust in his goodness and provision. He is a God who can be trusted, who will not fail.

With the prosperity we live in today, perhaps we struggle to relate to knowing God personally in this way. I have had glimpses of seeing the arm of the Lord in this way. When my husband and I were newly married, we moved into the inner city in London so that he could pastor a church there. The area was notorious for guns, gangs, and poverty. The church was a Victorian building that had been condemned by the authorities, and it was in serious need of repair. The congregation of one hundred or so came from a diverse spread of socioeconomic backgrounds, with many of them being employed young people not yet at the height of their earning power. In our first year we held a gift day after a few days of prayer and fasting. The amount we needed was five times more than any previous offering. The Saturday night before the service, one young couple woke in the night convinced that they needed to give the entire contents of one savings account. They had recently bought a house near the church that was in need of a new roof and had set aside the money when they completed the purchase. They donated the entire sum to the church. In the hours after the morning service, news of how generously this congregation had given reached the ears of the father of a friend of ours. He felt stirred to give the exact amount that was needed to meet the target. We did not ask him; God moved him, and on that gift day exactly enough money was given to repair the church.

"He has shown the strength of his arm." This is the truth. Mary knew it and she was able to declare it in faith.

To be a Christian is to know and experience God in this way—he shows the strength of his arm. Today, bring before him in prayer any needs that are known to you. May the strength of his arm be demonstrated and seen.

PRAYER

O LORD God Almighty, Father of angels and men,
We praise and bless your holy name for all your
goodness and loving kindness to humanity.
We bless you for our creation, preservation, and for
your unceasing generosity to us throughout our
lives; But above all, we bless you for your great love
in the redemption of the world by our Lord Jesus
Christ. We bless you for bringing us safe to the
beginning of a new day. Grant that this day we fall
into no sin, Neither run into any kind of danger. Keep
us, we pray, from all things hurtful to body or soul,
and grant us your pardon and peace, So that, being
cleansed from all our sins, We might serve you with
quiet hearts and minds, and continue in the same
until our life's end, through Jesus Christ, our Savior
and Redeemer. Amen.

John Wesley

The Crucifixion, a seventeenth century manuscript,
Tigray, Ethiopia. Photo by DeAgostini/Getty Images.

This picture is from a manuscript dating to the 1600s and kept in the museum of the Church of St. Mary of Zion Aksum (Unesco World Heritage List, 1980), in Tigray, Ethiopia. (Photo by DeAgostini/Getty Images.)

Some of the oldest churches, paintings, sculptures, and manuscripts in the world are found in Africa, which for several centuries was the heart of global Christian culture. Alexandria and Carthage were wealthy African cities in the Roman Empire and became centers of Christian thought and art. The church where this picture is housed was first built around 350 AD and was the traditional place for the coronation of Ethiopian kings. The image helps us to see a profoundly African faith depicted with all the figures having contextualized features, hair, and dress.

Mary sang of God *"performing mighty deeds with his arm"*— and here she is shown witnessing the ultimate fulfillment of this as Jesus's arms were stretched wide in his crucifixion. Here Mary, dressed in blue, seems to realize, in her despairing face, that the promise will be fulfilled in unexpected ways, as she gathers with others to see Jesus's sacrificial death.

He has scattered those who are proud in their inmost thoughts.

Luke 1:51

In Psalm 2, the psalmist asks, *"Why do the nations conspire, And the peoples plot in vain, The kings of the earth rise up, And the rulers band together?"* Mary was well versed in the Old Testament, and she seems to have had that scripture in mind when she said: *"He has scattered those who are proud in their inmost thoughts."* Mary lived at a time when her people and her homeland were subjugated by an arrogant and powerful empire. The outward displays of power were visible to see as occupying forces walked the streets and the need to pay taxes to Rome determined so much. But here Mary's words speak of more than military or political power. She addresses the human heart—the pride that lurks in secret in our inmost thoughts as human beings. It is this kind of pride that leads to a sense of superiority over others and that lies at the root of all abuses of power.

The proud and arrogant plot and scheme; they obsess about their power whether that means obtaining it or keeping it. Abuses and cover-ups are both rooted in pride. Mary reminds us that human pride and its schemes against what is good, right, beautiful, or true are nothing new. But God sees. Human beings may deflect or hide the pride of our inmost thoughts, but God sees all.

And here Mary prophesies that God will scatter the proud. The institutions and hierarchies of the proud will collapse; the perpetrators of harm and cover-up will be scattered. Mary composed her prophetic song while living under political oppression—she knew what it was to feel powerless—but with prophetic sight she was able to speak with confidence of a day when our God will do this. God will scatter the collective power of the arrogant.

God can judge and weigh our inmost thoughts. In 1944 a Hollywood movie titled *Gaslight* was released. In the film a husband slowly manipulates his wife into believing that she is slipping into insanity so as to distract her from his own wrongdoing. Mary's cry of hope that God will see and judge the inmost thoughts of the proud speaks to one of the deepest questions of our day.

The promise is that even the most hidden of hidden power abusers—the ultimate gaslighters who get us second-guessing ourselves with their clever machinations—will be scattered and stopped.

"He has scattered those who are proud in their inmost thoughts."

Mary speaks of God scattering proud people. This is more than scattering pebbles or seeds. It means to winnow or to throw up in the air, testing and shaking a harvest so as to dislodge and separate things. To scatter is to disperse, to rout, and to dislocate. It could also mean to shred, to confuse. The proud will be shaken and dispersed from community. In Mary's song there is a hope for a coming judgment upon the proud, and she looks to Jesus's coming as a promise that the current power structures will be upended.

In prophesying this judgment of the proud, Mary is echoing Hannah's song in 1 Samuel 2:3: "*Do not keep talking so proudly or let your mouth speak such arrogance, for the Lord is a God who knows, and by him deeds are weighed.*" God sees and knows all things. God weighs and judges our deeds. And Mary reminds us that God is not only the God of promises, but he is also the God of reversals. He sees the secret plans and schemes—the very thoughts of the proud. And he is able to subvert and prevent them—scattering and confusing their agendas. He will dismantle the systems that oppress and will unseat the proud from their positions of authority. Given the obscurity, poverty, disadvantage, and powerlessness of Mary and her people, this is a cry of hope.

As we read Mary's words of prophecy and hope today, our own relative positions of education, privilege, wealth, and opportunity make it difficult to see how the promises of judgment are good news. If we are well-fed, rich, respected, and upheld in positions of power, we may struggle to see the goodness and liberty promised in Mary's words.

Dietrich Bonhoeffer was a German pastor and theologian who was executed by the Nazis for his part in a plot on Hitler's life. He was caught between loyalty to his country and the need to resist the evil that had taken over in Germany. As a young pastor he used to host university students in his home to answer their questions and offer Christian hospitality in what he called "table talk." My grandfather attended meetings in his house as a university student in the 1920s. Bonhoeffer did resist the power structures of Nazism, and he called the Magnificat "the most passionate, the wildest, one might even say the most revolutionary hymn ever sung."[1]

To the lowly, the oppressed, the abused, the vulnerable, and the powerless, Mary's song is a cry of hope. And it is in tune with the heart of God throughout the scriptures. What Mary reveals about God here—*"He has scattered those who were proud in the thoughts of their heart"*—is one of the themes of the Old Testament. God has done this in the past, for example, facing down Pharaoh on his throne and making a way for the Israelites through the parting of the Red Sea. God crushed the Egyptians and humbled the Pharaoh. After delivering Goliath into David's hand, God scattered the Philistines. The pride of the nation is humbled and the army scatters. After delivering the three Hebrew young men who refused to bow to the Babylonian statue, God humbles the powerful king Nebuchadnezzar such that he believes he is an animal, and he is unable to wield power.

God is in the business of crushing pride and exalting humility—it's a form of justice. May our hearts thrill with hope that this is our God. May we turn from pride and look toward the coming justice of Jesus's Kingdom.

---

1 "The Mystery of Holy Night," *Dietrich Bonhoeffer's Christmas Sermons*, Zondervan, 2005.

PRAYER

Lord God
Give us true repentance;
forgive us our sins of negligence
and ignorance
and our deliberate sins;
and grant us the grace of your Holy Spirit
to amend our lives according to
your holy word.
Holy God,
holy and strong,
holy and immortal,
have mercy upon us. Amen.

The Church of England Book of Common Prayer

Red Thorns, Odilon Redon.

Odilon Redon was a French symbolist artist (1814–1916), born to a New Orleans French Creole mother. After serving in the French army he settled in Paris, where his style really began to take shape with swirling tableaus of color expressing his exploration of spiritual matters. Mary, clothed with a headscarf in this painting, had been warned that "a sword will pierce your own heart also." Here she is depicted with a crown of red thorns around her, resonant of the crown of thorns placed upon Jesus's head.

He has brought down rulers from their thrones.

Luke 1:52

The imagery Mary uses here is extremely potent. In the ancient world, one king would try to have a higher level of exaltation than the neighboring ruler. The way in which they measured their opulence was by the kind of throne that they established. How high was it? What was it made of? Was it made of ivory? Gold? Precious stones? Were the robes of the king more splendid than all the clothing that others might wear? They would use every one of these material symbols of power to project greatness. We do something similar in our culture with status symbols and the trappings of material wealth. But people who seek power seek what is temporary. The baubles and outward shows of power are ultimately empty and shallow; they are here today and gone tomorrow. God brings down rulers from their thrones.

The Greek word for ruler is *dunastas*, and it is rooted in the idea of power. We may not fear the traditional kings, presidents, mayors, congressional leaders, judges, or prime ministers who happen to exercise authority in the nations or neighborhoods we live in. This will be especially true if we live in freedom under a democracy. But there are other kinds of power closer to home.

The domestic bully who rules their household by instilling fear wields power by domination, intimidation, and their force of character. The family member who cannot be contradicted but must always be acquiesced to. The boss or leader of an organization who dearly loves the power that their position in the hierarchy gives them, whether that be through bestowing promotions or salary increases to those they deem loyal, or the threat of a negative review or loss of status for those who are out of favor. The threat of being smeared or having one's reputation tarnished or even destroyed hangs over those in the wake of people who hold power today. A ruler on a throne speaks of a dominator who evokes fear and perhaps of a petty person who regularly insists *I'm up here and you are down there*, if a co-worker outshines them. And then there are those who abuse others just because they can—sexually, psychologically, and physically.

Any of us who have been on the receiving end of power abuse will recognize the defiance of Mary's statement. Whether power was misused against us in the family we grew up in, the school we attended, the home we are building, the church we belonged to, the organization we work for, or the community infrastructure that we have trusted, it can shake us to the very core.

But Mary points us to a God of justice and truth, of goodness and beauty, and if we have been abused, taken advantage of, crushed, or trampled underfoot by ego, domination, or power of any sort, perhaps our hearts will thrill like Mary's did at the presence of the Lord and at the coming of Jesus. The Prince of Peace, Wonderful Counselor, and Mighty God. The one who can be trusted with power, the one who is for us. The one whose goodness will mean he brings "*down rulers from their thrones.*" Mary points us to a God who can be trusted with power in a world where power harms and hurts so many of us. We will not forever live subjugated to unjust power. Mary declares her hope in the promise that Jesus has come to rescue and deliver us from toxic uses of power in this world and in our lives.

One of the most traumatic experiences of my recent years was attending court for the criminal trial of a powerful person who had abused people sexually. Each evening after the day in court, I went and sat in the cathedral of the city where the case was being heard to attend evensong, a beautiful service of liturgy, choral music, and scripture reading. And each time I did, I was chilled to the bone when the choir sang the words of Mary's Magnificat and in particular "*He hath put down the mighty from their seats, and exalted them of low degree.*" A few months later, in a different cathedral when this experience was shared with a senior church leader, they expressed that it was fairly common for senior police officers, criminal lawyers, and judges to find their way to evensong amid the traumas of a trial. The hope of justice is a balm to the soul.

Dear friends who have lived through horrific persecution in their nations due to their Christian faith also find hope in these words. To have been imprisoned, assaulted, robbed, and shamed for following Christ, to have lost pastors, friends, and relatives to a murderous mob, still happens today. To experience this personally or to love those who live through such horrors leaves us longing for the day when God will bring down the powerful from their thrones.

Mary speaks for the vulnerable, the abused, and the hurting when she expresses her faith that God will bring down the powerful from their thrones. Mary warns us that this world is a place where power is abused, and she models disturbing, awakening, and mobilizing those of us who need to see the injustice around us and to take a stand. And for all of us as Christians, whether we find ourselves longing for justice on a personal level or not, this cry is central to the gospel, and it has been the hope of followers of Jesus since the earliest days of the faith. God will bring down any power, ruler, or stronghold whose throne is set up in opposition to Christ.

PRAYER

O Lord, open my eyes that I may see
the needs of others
Open my ears that I may hear their cries;
Open my heart so that they need not be
without succor;
Let me not be afraid to defend the weak because
of the anger of the strong,
Nor afraid to defend the poor because
of the anger of the rich.
Show me where love and hope and faith are needed,
And use me to bring them to those places.
And so open my eyes and my ears
That I may this coming day be able to do some
work of peace for thee.

Alan Paton (in *Acceptable Words: Prayers for the Writer* edited by
Gary D. Schmidt and Elizabeth Stickney, Eerdmans, 2012)

The Baptistry Ceiling, Florence, Italy.

Beginning in 1059 a magnificent set of church buildings was constructed in Florence, Italy. The first building was an octagonal church, called a Baptistry, where adults and children, including the famous poet Dante, were baptized into the Christian faith, surrounded by images of the core doctrines of the faith. Upon completion of the building, and over the course of about a hundred years, a series of golden mosaics were laid on the inside of the dome, so that those being baptized could look up and see them. Bible stories from both the Old and New Testaments are depicted. In the center, above the altar, is an image of the Last Judgment, with a figure of Christ as the Judge, whose arms stretch out to twenty-six feet, still showing the marks of the crucifixion. He is shown bringing an ultimate reckoning and reward. This is a dazzling and impressive display of a central truth in the heart of a town that was, at the time, one of the most powerful in the world. The image reminds us that above all human power, there is God, in Christ, showing love and acceptance to the downtrodden, and a reckoning to the powerful on their thrones.

But he has lifted up the humble.

Luke 1:52

Mary's word points us to a God who lifts up the humble and who is humble himself. This care for the humble is in stark contrast with the culture of Mary's age and the influencers of our day. In her womb, Mary carries the one who created the universe, but went on to say in his teaching: *"Learn from me, for I am gentle and humble in heart, and you will find rest for your souls"* (Matthew 11:29).

There is no prioritizing of the strategic, the significant, the honored, or the influential. God is in the business of lifting up the humble. The whole ministry of Jesus as recorded in the gospels is an outworking of this—to the broken, the bruised, the humble, and the hurting. Jesus is described in Matthew 12:20 as being the one the prophet Isaiah saw as a coming Messiah. *"A bruised reed he will not break and a faintly burning wick he will not quench; he will faithfully bring forth justice."*

What does lifting up the humble really look like? The theologian Kenneth Bailey lived in the Middle East for sixty years. He notes that reeds in the Middle East are not thin stems used for flower arranging. Reeds are huge, towering structural plants, and in the ancient world they were used for the construction of things like houses and boats. They could carry great weight. However, if the reed became bruised, it was utterly useless—in fact it would be dangerous to use it as it would not be able to hold the weight of anything resting on it. Out of concern for safety, a bruised reed would be broken up and destroyed by fire so that no one could mistake it for something useful.

The Messiah, by refusing to "break the bruised reed," would be an astonishing person. The Messiah might take and redeem lives that were utterly broken and useless—good for nothing but destruction. This is underscored by the other image used here by Isaiah. The Messiah will not snuff out a smoldering wick. In houses made of reeds there was a high risk of fire—that meant that under every oil lamp a pan of water waited so that when a wick was burned up and fully used, instead of falling onto the floor it fell through the lamp into water. This is a smoldering wick—a completely useless and used-up wick. The Messiah will not snuff out such a wick.

The bruised and broken need to hear that God will lift up the humble. Any person who feels disappointed in themselves, bruised, humiliated, shamed, and without hope can listen to the defiant, joyous Advent proclamation of Mary: *"But he has lifted up the humble."*

Mary's words were unexpected and subversive at the time she spoke them. We may be used to thinking of a humble heart as a positive thing. But the ancient world treated humility as a weakness to be avoided rather than a virtue to be aspired to. Regardless of whether you were rich or poor, what was most important was *honor*—having your status, connections, and merits recognized and your name praised. This meant that boasting about achievements was expected in the Greco-Roman world, and those with merit should seek to honor themselves whenever possible. Humility was not in the least bit positive—it was seen as something for children and slaves, and actually dishonorable for adult men and women. Promoting your own honor was taken for granted, as honor was your greatest asset and shame your worst fear. Humility was only practiced before the powerful because they could kill you. To be humble with your equal or someone of lesser status was seen as morally suspect.

Mary, by speaking of a God who lifts up and loves the humble, is prophesying something countercultural and profound in her moment in history. In fact, the life of Jesus would go on to fundamentally change how humility was seen from that time onward. When the Son of God willingly submitted to the most humiliating act the Romans could concoct—crucifixion. Jesus conquered evil, sin, and death by laying down his life. He called those who follow him to lay down our lives in service of him. Because of that we can see humility not as a weakness but as a virtue.

My husband and I pastored a church in the inner city in London for seven years. The neighborhood was known for gun and gang violence. But at the core of the church was a group of women who had come to the UK in the 1950s from the Caribbean. They had experienced tremendous hardship, including racism and financial difficulties. Without fail, every Thursday evening for over fifty years they prayed in a prayer meeting lifting up the church and the surrounding community to the Lord. The church experienced wonderful growth, and many young people came to Christ. His Royal Highness King Charles III (then the Prince of Wales) came to visit the church. The main meeting he had was with this group of women. The king of the United Kingdom heard their stories and thanked them for their faithfulness. It was a wonderful picture of a bigger truth—that the King of Kings will lift high the humble.

Mary's words of prophecy about what her son's life would mean include this promise: "*He has lifted up the humble.*" If you are bruised or broken, Jesus will not discard or ignore you. He showed us a different way of living, a different value system, and he offers that hope today.

PRAYER

God of compassion whose son Jesus Christ, the
child of Mary, shared the life of a home in Nazareth,
and on the cross drew the whole human family
to himself, strengthen us in our daily living that in
joy and in sorrow, we may know the power of your
presence, to bind together and to heal through
Jesus Christ our Lord. Amen.

The Church of England Book of Common Prayer

Giotto, Cathedral Church (1311–20), Assisi.

Giotto painted these panels in the Cathedral Church (or Basilica) of Assisi, in Italy. It is said that the large congregations, which had begun to gather as a result of the ministry of St. Francis of Assisi, meant that the small chapels with dark interiors would no longer serve the needs of people who wanted to hear sermons and the scriptures read out and explained. The larger buildings were decorated using the fresco method, and have, after some restoration, been returned to the clear lines and bright colors that better represented the sense of humility Francis was able to recapture as the churches were reformed and reinvigorated.

There is an essential fragility here: a young mother cradling her baby, riding an ass, being led by Joseph into the uncertainty of exile and refugee status in Egypt. Joseph looks back, concerned for their well-being, amid a setting of the countryside, with the safety of the towns with city wall retreating into the distance. The damaged writing reed and the smoldering lamp wick are usually disposed of, as they no longer serve their purpose, but human beings are infinitely more precious in the eyes of God. One angel looks back into the past of a child born in an outbuilding under the threat of genocide, and the other seems to gaze, concerned, into the future of refugee status and perhaps a certain death, and yet here is the mystery of the longed-for Redeemer. No wonder Peter says *"angels long to gaze on such things"* (1 Peter 1:12).

He has filled the hungry with good things but has sent the rich away empty.

Luke 1:53

Here Mary looks forward to the promise of Christ's coming and considers what it will mean for those who are hungry. The word *hungry* could mean those who are famished, or who crave something, who are needy or who earnestly desire fulfillment in some way.

Happiness, or a sense of fulfillment, in today's world is often seen as being wrapped up in our human pursuit of fullness—full health, full bank accounts, full social life, and a life full of hobbies. We are surrounded by the pursuit of the materialist dream. We are pursuing affluence, but we are experiencing emptiness. Yet the good things that God has given us on this earth are so much more than the American dream. When we mistake good things for the real thing we as humans most ultimately desire, our Creator himself, we will find ourselves empty and disappointed. C. S. Lewis points out that idols inevitably break the hearts of their worshippers in his book *The Weight of Glory*. He writes: "These things—the beauty, the memory of our own past—are good images of what we really desire; but if they are mistaken for the thing itself, they turn into dumb idols, breaking the hearts of their worshipers. For they are not the thing itself; they are only the scent of a flower we have not found, the echo of a tune we have not heard, news from a country we have never yet visited."[1]

In fact, Mary warns us that wealth and its pursuit can keep us from truly experiencing and receiving the fullness of what God offers. It is only if we are hungry that we can be filled by God with good things. If we believe we are already full, we can't receive this other kind of fullness that Mary speaks of. There is a poignancy here. The fullness of joy that Jesus gives is in stark contrast to the emptiness experienced by those who may be materially rich. Studies of affluence seem to uphold this: the data shows that the more we pursue consumerism, status, and the accumulation of wealth, the unhappier and emptier we have become. Mary points us to God in Christ as the one who can fill our hearts with truly good things—hope, promise, joy, and forgiveness. As Jesus himself puts it: *"Blessed are those who hunger and thirst for righteousness for they will be filled"* (Matthew 5:6).

Mary is highlighting the truth that the persistent hunger of the human heart will lead us toward God. The desire points beyond itself to the fulfillment of that desire—and so this kind of hunger is actually a gift enabling us to receive the good things that can satisfy it. On a very simple level we may

---

1   C. S. Lewis's sermon, "The Weight of Glory," first preached in the University Church of St. Mary the Virgin on June 8, 1941. It was published in *Theology* 43 (November 1941): 263–274, and then as *The Weight of Glory* (New York: Macmillan 1949).

experience this in our bodies. We may become so stressed and frenetic that we are out of touch with our hunger, unable to face eating any food. It is only when we stop for a moment, breathe deeply, and think about needing to eat that we may have the wherewithal to find something to eat and begin to feel better. A parent of a toddler knows the moment when the child has gone beyond the point of hunger and the meltdown or tantrum is inevitable. At that point it will take a lot more energy, persuasion, and patience to give the child what they need. Recognizing and attuning ourselves to hunger is a parenting necessity and a life skill. Spiritual hunger is the same—it needs to be acknowledged and validated. It can only be satisfied once discerned and brought to God.

In *Mere Christianity*, C. S. Lewis wrote: "Creatures are not born with desires unless satisfaction for those desires exists. A baby feels hunger: well, there is such a thing as food. A duckling wants to swim: well, there is such a thing as water....If I find in myself a desire which no experience in this world can satisfy, the most probable explanation is that I was made for another world. If none of my earthly pleasures satisfy it, that does not prove that the universe is a fraud. Probably earthly pleasures were never meant to satisfy it, but only to arouse it, to suggest the real thing."[1]

The rich, who believe themselves to be full, are found to be empty. The very wealth that our culture tells us to pursue in order to feel happy, safe, and fulfilled ends up leaving us empty,

---

1 C. S. Lewis, *Mere Christianity* (London: HarperCollins, 2015), pp. 135–137.

exhausted, and sad. This chimes with the experiences of many in our culture. Anxiously acquiring wealth leads to more stress; the more we consume the less satisfied we seem to be.

Mary's answer is hunger. Be hungry, express hunger to God. Ask God to fill your hunger with truly good things.

Why not acknowledge your hunger today and turn toward the one who can satisfy our deepest longings in this Advent season? After all, he is called the Desire of Nations. Jesus is the fulfillment of the desires of all the nations on earth. The only qualification Mary mentions for receiving the "good things" he offers us is to be hungry.

PRAYER

Almighty God,
who wonderfully created us in your own image
and yet more wonderfully restored us
through your Son Jesus Christ:
grant that, as he came to share in our humanity,
so we may share the life of his divinity;
who is alive and reigns with you,
in the unity of the Holy Spirit,
one God, now and for ever. Amen.

The Church of England Book of Common Prayer

The Virgin and Child, c. 800 AD.
Artist: Unknown.

The *Book of Kells* is sometimes known as the *Book of Columba*. It is a Celtic illustrated manuscript and is considered by many to be one of Ireland's most significant national treasures. The manuscript contains the four gospels in Latin with an introduction, and it dates to around the year 800. The beautiful calligraphy and illumination throughout the book include this image of Mary with Jesus. Mary is clothed in the native Irish saffron veil and a more imperial purple robe. Her facial features are notably Celtic, making her identifiable as a mother, but she is also haloed as a reminder that she is the Mother of Christ. This depiction of Mary is the only image of a woman that appears in the entire book. Jesus is depicted as a small adult, and he looks into his mother's face. Angels are painted in each corner of the image. Three angels hold a flabellum—a metal disk mounted on a handle that was used in liturgical services at the time. This hints at the Eucharist: the Christ Child will provide food for the community of the faithful, and Mary was the tabernacle that brought him to birth. Through Christ, Mary's prophecy that the hungry will be satisfied is fulfilled.

He has helped his servant Israel, remembering to be merciful to Abraham and his descendants forever, just as He promised our ancestors.

Luke 1:54–55

Mary lands and grounds her Magnificat in remembering the promises to her own people that were given over many generations and recorded in the Old Testament. Scholars note that Jesus is the fulfillment of more than one hundred Old Testament messianic prophecies made to the Jewish people. Mary closes her song of praise by rooting everything that she's been saying up to this point in the historical expectation of the Messiah in the Old Testament. The coming of Jesus as the anointed one is not an unexpected random event. Mary now declares her conviction that the time of waiting is over—her pregnancy is the fulfillment of the many promises made to her ancestors.

Perhaps you have experienced the frustration of waiting for something for a very long time, even for years. It can be hard to keep on hoping when it feels like the thing you have expected or hoped for keeps being delayed. It can even be painful and damaging to a relationship if somebody has promised you something that they forget to do or if delays block the resolution of a desired outcome. I have seen this in business transactions and even in court cases where procedural delays drag out a just outcome for years and years. I have seen friends go through long periods of infertility when it becomes harder and harder to hope for a longed-for child. In Mary's time, the people of God had been waiting for centuries for the fulfillment of their promised deliverance. It must have been tempting to give up. To get on with life and stop hoping. Mary's words cut through the desolation of waiting. *He has helped* and *He has remembered.*

"*He has helped his servant Israel.*" Mary reminds us that the Psalmist who lived hundreds of years before her spoke of God as the helper of Israel on numerous occasions. "*Because you are my help, I sing in the shadow of your wings*" (Psalm 63:7). There was already an established pattern of singing to God as our help, and Mary consciously positions her song in this tradition.

The key theme of this last phrase of Mary's song is God's remembering—this is a reference to his faithfulness. It carries an active sense of God doing what he has said he will do rather than just remembering as a form of calling things to mind. Mary speaks of God "*Remembering to be merciful to Abraham and his descendants, just as He promised*" as a description of his actions in giving the Savior of the world as a child in her womb.

But Mary's worship isn't focused on herself or even on her own role in the promises of God—significant as it is. Mary is praising God because she realizes that the time has finally arrived for the sending of the longed-for Savior of the world.

"The help" has arrived and God is fulfilling his promises of many generations.

The Messianic promises that she may be calling to mind here could include the promise to Eve that her seed would put an end to evil and bruise the serpent's head. Mary mentions the promises to Abraham—he was promised that the son born in his old age would be the father of a nation through which all the nations of the world would be blessed. Abraham was also promised that God would provide a ram for the sacrifice he had been asked to make at the top of Mount Moriah. Hundreds of years later Mary's son would climb the same mountain, carrying the wood for his own crucifixion just as Isaac carried the wood. Jesus's sacrifice would be for the sins of the world. Unlike Abraham, Mary would not see her son spared; Jesus was to be the provision from God, the lamb of God, given for the sins of the world.

Mary notes that God remembers his promises—perhaps she is referring to the promise to Moses that God would send a prophet greater than him to the people. Or the promise to David that his descendant would reign forever and that the nations would be his inheritance. Or the promise to Isaiah that a baby would be born in history whose name would be Wonderful Counselor, Mighty God, Everlasting Father, Prince of Peace. Or the promise to Daniel that one "like a Son of Man" would come in glory from the right hand of God. Or the promise to Hosea that the Messiah would be brought up out of Egypt, or the promise to Micah that the Messiah would be born in Bethlehem or the promise to Zechariah that the Messiah would be pierced.

God had been promising the coming of a savior for generations, and Mary knew that the time had now come. God has remembered his promises. And she includes herself as one who is in need of the promise—she notes her own involvement in all of this with the phrase "*our ancestors*." Mary is not a disinterested bystander. She acknowledges that the longing and hope of her people, of her ancestors involves her. A humble, unknown woman gets to be a part of God's promises in human history.

Don't give up hope. Our God is a God who remembers, who knows, who helps. In this Advent season as we prepare our minds and hearts to worship Christ, marveling that he came into this world and was born for our salvation, surrender to him again your hopes and cares.

PRAYER

Almighty and everlasting God, you are always more ready to hear than we are to pray, and you are willing to give more than either we desire or deserve—pour down upon us the abundance of your mercy, forgiving us those things of which our consciences are afraid, and giving to us that which our prayers dare not presume to ask; through Jesus Christ our Lord. Amen.

The Church of England Book of Common Prayer

Marc Chagall, *Abraham and Isaac*, Nice, France.

Marc Chagall, a twentieth-century French painter with a Russian and Jewish background, is best known for his paintings on biblical and scriptural themes. Chagall's notably colorful and free style of work successfully tied together narrative vignettes that blend eras. In this picture, Abraham's son Isaac is about to be sacrificed when God intervenes through an angel to stop this occurring. A portal to the future takes us to the cross, where another son bore the wood for his own sacrifice, and where Mary mirrors the motherly concern of her forebear Sarah. Abraham declares the promise "God will provide a lamb," and Jesus is later called the "lamb of God who takes away the sin of the world"—this little phrase is recollected by a small blue lamb under a tree. Chagall makes every effort to represent all the major color blocks in his palette—building on a dreamlike white background, and cycling through primary hues of green, blue, yellow, and red, as if to emphasize the theological completion represented in this moment for generations to come.

And she gave birth to her firstborn, a son.

Luke 2:7

The Son is the image of the invisible God, the firstborn over all creation.

Colossians 1:15

I wonder how much birth order matters to you. When you think about your place in your family, does it matter when you were born in comparison to other brothers and sisters? In our family the twin boys know that one is older than the other by only one minute. He calls it "the golden minute." But the second boy loves the fact that in Nigeria a second-born twin is seen as the leader, the primary child, because he or she pushed their sibling out into the world first ahead of them to check that everything is fine, before coming out themselves.

In chapter 2 of Luke's gospel, the author makes a point of saying Mary gave birth to her firstborn, a son. Mary is the source for this detail. This is significant because Jesus is the firstborn in more ways than one. It is important because it emphasizes that Mary was a virgin who gave birth to Jesus because Jesus is God incarnate—his conception was a miracle in which the Holy Spirit caused Mary's egg to be fertilized so that a fully human child who was also fully God could be born. There is no confusion here about Jesus's identity.

This is also important because the firstborn in an ancient culture carried the entire hopes, substance, authority, and potential of a family. Jesus carries the very being and nature of God into human history as he takes on flesh to dwell among us. The New Testament describes him as the *firstborn over all creation*. "*Everything was made by him and for him*" (Colossians 1:16, NLV), and yet he enters his own creation as a baby. St. Augustine captures the contrasts of Jesus's authority and vulnerability in his status as the firstborn: "He who made man became man; he was formed in the Mother who He Himself formed, carried in the hands which He made, nourished at the breasts which He filled; that in the manger in mute infancy, He the Word, without whom all human eloquence is mute wailed."[1] This title of firstborn encapsulates the mystery of the incarnation because it speaks of the earthiness of Jesus's birth alongside the majesty of his status and authority in the cosmos.

All parents will also know that the first birth a woman experiences is usually the most difficult on a physical level. Jesus is the only Son of God, and he is the firstborn son of Mary. She has no experience to draw on, and she seems to be far away from her closest relatives—since she needed to travel to Bethlehem to be with her husband's people for the census. This emphasis on the word *firstborn* is a statement about Mary.

---

1   Saint Augustine, Sermon 188, 2.

God calls a young, inexperienced girl who could never earn her role or qualify herself for the task. Her tremendous vulnerability is matched by his own—as Jesus comes into this world as a baby. This is how God reveals himself, who he is and what he is like. He shows himself to be humble, gentle, and lowly. He is born in obscurity and relative poverty to be nurtured, fed, raised, and protected by an untested teenage girl. Jesus is the firstborn son of Mary and the firstborn over all creation.

The location of Jesus's birth in Bethlehem is now commemorated with a beautiful church, attracting thousands of visitors every year with a gilded star marking the spot within where it is believed Mary actually gave birth. When I visited, I was struck by the physicality of it all. God was born in a specific place and time in human history and geography. Birth is a visceral and messy business. And that speaks to the reality of our lives. God meets us as human beings—not in theory but in reality.

In this Advent season, we have the opportunity to try to grasp the wonder of this cosmic mystery—that God came into this world as a firstborn son, born of a virgin. The Lord of all, the creator of galaxies and planets, was born; he lay in his mother's arms as a tiny baby. Her first baby. The wonder of the incarnation is something so beautiful and so powerful and truly paradoxical. Stop for a moment in the busyness of the buildup to Christmas and take a pause to wonder at the truth that Jesus is the firstborn over creation.

PRAYER

Almighty God, you have given us your only
begotten Son to take our nature upon him,
and to be born of a virgin—grant that we, being
regenerate and made your children by adoption
and grace, may daily be renewed by your Holy Spirit,
through the same, our Lord Jesus Christ,
who lives and reigns with you and the Holy Spirit,
world without end. Amen.

The Church of England Book of Common Prayer

Virgin and Child with Angels, National Gallery, London.

This startling blue painting is part of a small and rare English altar piece from 1395 to 1399 called the "Wilton Diptych." It was painted for the monarch, King Richard II, and it opens up from outer layers to show this scene.

The blue pigment is especially vibrant and was made from mixing the semiprecious stone *lapis lazuli* with egg white, and the oak board is covered in gold leaf. One of the challenges for art in the Christian tradition is the need to show natural and spiritual realities simultaneously, and this artist stacks up angels into the distance. The infant Jesus in Mary's arms is centered as the true King and he is reaching out to bless those who are painted, one of whom is a portrait of King Richard II himself. Christ is both a child born to a human mother Mary, and the firstborn over all creation. The expense of the materials used and the homage of an earthly king pay tribute to this truth.

So Joseph also went up from the town of Nazareth in Galilee, to Judea, to Bethlehem, the town of David, because he belonged to the house and line of David. He went there to register with Mary, who was pledged to be married to him and was expecting a child. While they were there the time came for the baby to be born.

Luke 2:4–6

A shoot will come up from the stump of Jesse; from his roots a Branch will bear fruit.

Isaiah 11:1

At Advent, we reflect on the meaning of the coming of God in Christ into human history. Jesus was born in the city of David, Bethlehem, and into David's family. The Old Testament describes a shoot growing out of an old stump. The stump is the remainder of a severely pruned or cut-down tree. And this stump is "of Jesse." Jesse was David's father. A shoot would suddenly spring up in the line of Jesse and will "bear fruit." Jesus's birth in Bethlehem is a fulfillment of this hope.

My husband and I have a small farm where we practice conservation. Historically this farm was a fruit farm growing cherries and plums for the city of London. When we purchased the property, it had fallen into serious disrepair and the orchards had not been pruned for decades. Most of the trees had not produced fruit for decades either. Yet from seemingly dead trees, shoots do suddenly appear, taking us by surprise. In the year after we first saw the farm, some of the plum trees burst back into life. There were a few branches that had so many plums appear on them that they snapped off under the weight of all the fruit and fell to the ground. That is the visual image that Isaiah deploys, promising that a Messiah would come in the line of Jesse: *"A shoot will come up from the stump of Jesse; from his roots a Branch will bear fruit."*

Mary had traveled with her betrothed to Bethlehem and the time had come to have this baby while they happened to be there. Although Bethlehem is a small town, it is known as the City of David. It was David's family home. In the Old Testament, Bethlehem is mentioned as the place where the prophet Samuel recognizes David and then anoints him as king (1 Samuel 16:1–16). David was the first king of Israel, and he represents the prophetic and spiritual hopes and expectations of a coming Messiah. The Messiah would be a son of David, and the dream of every generation of God's people was that he would restore the identity and glory of his people.

The name *Bethlehem* means "House of Bread," which alludes to a broader theme of provision of food and Jesus as he later describes himself as "The Bread of Life." But on a practical level, Bethlehem was surrounded by bountiful fields that supplied plentiful grain, despite being in the Judean desert.

The town is situated about five miles southwest of Jerusalem in the hill country of Judah, and it sits at about twenty-five hundred feet above sea level. The climate is mild, and the rainfall is plentiful. Bethlehem signifies fertile fields, orchards, and vineyards.

Mary knew the scriptures and so she would have known the history of King David and the prophecies of a new Davidic king who would one day lead God's people out of bondage back to true worship of him, and to coherence and success as a people. She may have known of the Prophet Micah's words: *"But you, Bethlehem Ephrathah, though you are small among the clans of Judah, out of you will come for me one who will be ruler over Israel, whose origins are from of old, from ancient times"* (Micah 5:2). These words linked the Messianic hope of God's people with the geographical location of Bethlehem.

Jesus is the fulfillment of an ultimate hope—a longing that God would come in history, and this unfolds in a specific way. By fulfilling prophecy in such a way, God reassures and confirms to us that this is a hope that is reliable and trustworthy. Jesus is also the subject of our hope. He will *"bear much fruit."* Any of us who long for meaning and are looking for order and purpose in this chaotic world can look to Jesus, the root of Jesse, the desire of the nations, the firstborn of a virgin woman named Mary in first-century Bethlehem, and he can restore our hope.

The fields that surround Bethlehem where the shepherds met angels on the day of Jesus's birth are the same fields that a man named Boaz once owned. This is where he met Ruth on the threshing floor. The book of Ruth describes how she as a poor woman gleaned grain in the fields of Boaz, eventually going on to meet and marry him. That same location—the fields around Bethlehem—became the place of the conception of King David's grandfather. It is no accident that Jesus was born in this place, and that shepherds who were now working in Boaz's lands meet angels in that exact place who tell them, "*Today in the town of David, a Savior has been born to you; he is the Messiah, the Lord*" (Luke 2:11).

The details of the location—Bethlehem—add such richness to the text and it reminds us, and Mary, that this birth is no accident. God's coming in human history is beautifully and intricately designed. This points us to hope. The hope of a nation—the longed-for Messiah—was fulfilled in the birth of Jesus in Bethlehem. In this Advent season, Bethlehem can stand as a reminder for us of hope. Hope that the promises of God in all their richness and detail can be trusted.

PRAYER

Jesus, brightness of your Father,
guide every event in our lives
for your highest purpose
and for our good,
until we arrive in your house,
and stand before your throne;
you live and reign, now and forever. Amen.

The Church of England Book of Common Prayer

Marc Chagall, *Ruth Galaneuse*,
private collection, London.

Ruth is one of the heroines of the Old Testament. Though originally a foreigner, once widowed she accompanies her mother-in-law back to her origins in Bethlehem. This evocative print blends a form of romanticism with the rural colors of ripe fields and gleaning. To glean was to pick up remaining pieces of wheat after the harvesters had gone through. What began as a work of kindness from a wealthy landowner, named Boaz, to a destitute young woman becomes a love story, which ultimately brings a thread of redemption into the family. Bethlehem is a recurring destination for the actions of God, later the town of King David, and later still the place of Jesus's birth. Ruth is sketched out, tall and resplendent in red, shimmering with her shoulders piled high with golden food. She is Mary's forebear, and she is depicted bringing home food to share with her despairing mother-in-law Naomi, who has slumped on the ground in front of her. Chagall captures the pathos of the scene with his use of color and simple lines.

But Mary treasured up all these things and pondered them in her heart.

Luke 2:19

Mary is the eyewitness to the account that Luke has written down. It is important to her that this detail of her treasuring details and pondering them is noted amid the whirlwind of activity that the story of the birth of Jesus entails as recorded by Luke and Matthew. The seismic events surrounding the birth of the savior involve fast-moving activity including prophecy, annunciation by an angel, a visit to relatives near Jerusalem, miraculous conception, a long journey, a birth far from home, angelic visitation, visits from shepherds, a dream, and an escape to Egypt. In the midst of these life-changing activities, Mary is a person who takes note of details. The lack of space in the home they hoped to stay in, the type of clothing the baby wore after birth, the need to place him in a manger (an animal food trough) as there was no cradle.

"But Mary treasured up all these things and pondered them in her heart."

The events occurred but were not forgotten, the historical record is accurately preserved. But Mary also believed that there was meaning, and profound theological truth, to be found in her experiences. She treasured "all these things." The Greek word for "treasured," *syneterei*, also means "kept safe." Elsewhere, *treasured* is translated as *dieterei*, meaning "to keep carefully." With *syneterei*, we see Mary keeping the details of Jesus's birth and the meaning of his coming safe.

It is the angels who proclaim the good news of the birth of the child who is Immanuel—God with us. By contrast Mary does not proclaim at this stage. Instead, she treasures the details in her heart and ponders. Luke makes this point twice for emphasis. The first time we hear that Mary treasured these things about Jesus in her heart was after she had been visited by the shepherds who came to the place where she had given birth in order to worship her son.

The second time that we hear of Mary treasuring or pondering things in her heart was when she and Joseph found Jesus talking to the teachers in the temple as a child. As parents they reprimanded him, as they had lost track of where he was, and he answered, "*'Why were you searching for me?'...'Didn't you know I had to be in my Father's house?'*" The text goes on to explain "*But they did not understand what he was saying to them. Then he went down to Nazareth with them and was obedient to them. But his mother treasured all these things in her heart*" (Luke 2:49–51).

Mary was a woman of activity, obedience, and practicality. She gave birth to a child in difficult circumstances, noting the details and remembering every aspect of what had happened and showing herself to be an accurate, reliable witness of the facts. Mary cared for the particulars of the narrative; she took time to memorize, reflect upon, and capture detail. But Mary was also a person of deep faith, theological insight, biblical knowledge, and rich experience. She pondered and reflected upon the meaning of what had happened.

Mary treasured the details of what had unfolded, actively remembering and reflecting on what had been revealed to her through Gabriel and through the Holy Scriptures. She placed value on revelation, and so she plays an extraordinary role in salvation history as the primary historical witness to the incarnation of God. One of the definitions of the word *treasured* is "to preserve a thing from perishing or being lost." It is extraordinary to realize that it is not only Mary who treasures truth. God chose her. God entrusted the most precious revelation of himself—the birth of Jesus—in history to a young woman. This speaks of who God is. Who he treasures, who is included, who he can use, and who he calls to be a witness.

Mary was steeped in the scriptures; she committed details to memory, and she became the greatest female witness in history. Her role as *theotokos*—the mother of God—is in part a role of witness. And so, she treasures up all these things and ponders them.

The Christian life is a beautiful combination of treasuring and witnessing. We are called as followers of Jesus to do both—to ponder and to proclaim. All too easily our heroes fall into one of either category. Those who are gifted to communicate, to proclaim, to connect. Or those who excel in contemplating, musing, wondering, uncovering depth of insight. We can easily find ourselves boxed into a branch of Christian faith that emphasizes one over the other. But Mary is a model of a person who both treasures and ponders, who retreats and reflects but who also works, moves, acts, and proclaims.

In this Advent season may we also be inspired to both—to ponder and to proclaim.

PRAYER

Great and glorious God, and Thou Lord Jesus,
I pray you shed abroad your light in the
darkness of my mind. Be found of me, Lord,
so that in all things I may act only in
accordance with Thy holy will. Amen.

Francis of Assisi

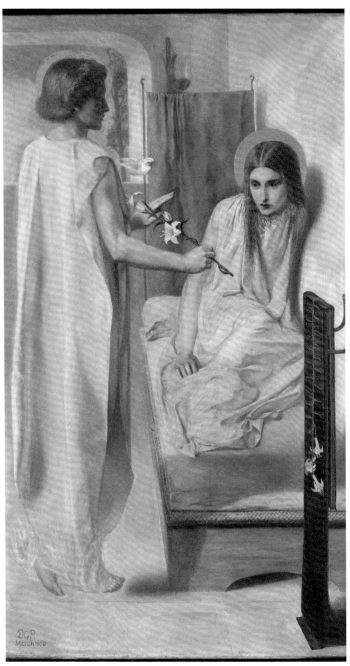

Ecce Ancilla Domini (*Behold the Handmaid of the Lord*),
Dante Gabriel Rossetti, 1850.

The pre-Raphaelites saw themselves as philosophical and artistic revolutionaries; they sought to rescue sacred art from the realm of fantasy and turned toward a new spiritual and physical realism. Their attention to detail went as far as the fine precision of selecting specific individuals for their life drawings. In this picture Gabriel is the artist's brother, William, and Mary is modeled by Rossetti's sister, Christina. He paints Mary as pensive, chiming with the description of her in Luke's text as engaging with theology and pondering many things in her heart. The Angel Gabriel is demystified; the only tokens of his angelic status are small flames, which lift him a few inches from the floor, and a gentle halo. The recurring white hues, in walls, dress, lilies, and the dove, are meant to remind us of the reality of Mary's youth and virginity.

On the eighth day, when it was time to circumcise the child, he was named Jesus, the name the angel had given him before he was conceived.

Luke 2:21

When they had gone, an angel of the Lord appeared to Joseph in a dream. "Get up," he said, "take the child and his mother and escape to Egypt. Stay there until I tell you, for Herod is going to search for the child to kill him." So he got up, took the child and his mother during the night and left for Egypt, where he stayed until the death of Herod. And so was fulfilled what the Lord had said through the prophet: "Out of Egypt I called my son."

Matthew 2:13–15

Eight days after his birth, Mary and Joseph ensure that Jesus was circumcised and named. This small detail is telling. Jesus will be raised in the customs and traditions of the Jewish people inspired by the Old Testament scriptures. But it is also an act of vulnerability.

This is the only record that we have about the circumcision of Jesus, just this one sentence that on the eighth day, according to the law, they brought Him to be circumcised. This is a reference to the teaching of the Mosaic law. Part of God's covenant with Abraham was the practice of the circumcision of all the male children. God had called Abraham when he was ninety-nine years old and said to him that his children would be as numerous as the stars in the heavens and the sands on the shore. Great nations will come from him, and through his seed, all the families of the earth would be blessed. Circumcision of every Jewish male was a part of the covenanted relationship between God and with the children of Abraham forever.

Mary's son is born as the Messiah of the Jewish people; he is to be the ultimate fulfillment of the promises to Abraham, and as such Jesus will fulfill all righteousness according to the Mosaic Law: his circumcision on the eighth day and being presented to the Temple on the fortieth day, with His parents making the proper sacrifices.

Jesus keeps all the requirements of the law and goes on to say, "*I have come, not to break the law, but to fulfil it...not one jot or tittle of the law will pass away, until all things are fulfilled.*" Jesus's circumcision points forward to his crucifixion. When all the requirements of the law have been perfectly upheld by him and he is crucified for the sins of the world, Jesus's last word is *tetelestai.* "*It is finished.*" It is complete. That means that the Mosaic Law is fulfilled and perfected. Nothing more is needed than to believe in Jesus because he has perfected everything.

Circumcision is an act of extreme vulnerability before God. It happens with the shedding of blood. It points forward to the self-sacrifice of Jesus prefiguring his self-emptying on the cross, when he's pierced with a sword and bleeds blood and water. The circumcision of Jesus is a prefiguration of his crucifixion.

The circumcision of the savior locates him as the hope of Israel, showing Mary's faith in God is rooted in the Old Testament promise and covenant with her forefathers. She sees Jesus as the fulfillment of the scriptures and understands her own role in that light.

The vulnerability of the family is also brought into view by Matthew's gospel, where Joseph is warned in a dream that they need to leave Bethlehem for their own safety. Having traveled from Nazareth to Bethlehem due to the geo-political situation, they now flee to Egypt for their own safety. Joseph "took the mother and her child." The precarious situation of this new mother is somehow emphasized in these words. Mary and Jesus are not safe. They need to flee to a neighboring country. Many people experience this need to uproot and flee in our world. My family and I have welcomed two women who were fleeing conflict in Ukraine to stay with us. The fear and trauma are etched on their faces. My father's earliest childhood memories relate to fleeing Soviet occupation with his own parents.

After all that Mary has experienced thus far, she now moves and lives in a foreign land as a refugee. Jesus the savior of the world is born into the fragility and vulnerability of this upheaval. In this Advent season as we experience the vulnerability and lack of safety involved in living in this world, we reflect on our savior who did not avoid this turmoil himself. Who was circumcised as one of his own people, identifying with the law and promises given to Israel, and who was taken with his family to flee as a refugee into a neighboring land, experiencing the trauma, hazard, and uncertainty of upheaval.

PRAYER

O Wisdom of our God Most High,
guiding creation with power and love:
come to teach us the path of knowledge!
O Leader of the House of Israel,
giver of the Law to Moses on Sinai:
come to rescue us with your mighty power!
O Root of Jesse's stem,
sign of God's love for all his people:
come to save us without delay!
O Key of David,
opening the gates of God's eternal Kingdom:
come and free the prisoners of darkness!
O Radiant Dawn,
splendor of eternal light, sun of justice:
come and shine on those who dwell in
darkness and in the
shadow of death.
O Dayspring, splendour of light eternal
and sun of righteousness:
Come and enlighten those who dwell in darkness
and the shadow of death.
O King of all nations and keystone of the Church:
come and save man, whom you formed
from the dust!
O Emmanuel, our King and Giver of Law:
come to save us, Lord our God!

The Anglican Service Book

Samuel Palmer, *Repose of the Holy Family*,
Ashmolean Museum, Oxford.

Samuel Palmer was a contemporary of William Blake, and they were both part of a group of artists who called themselves "The Ancients." They wanted to engage again with older forms of faith, art, and beauty in the first half of the 1800s, when industrialization was changing life and landscapes all around them in London and Kent. Palmer deploys complex techniques with texture and color in a near tropical and imagination-rich landscape setting, yet the Holy Family resting in the bottom right-hand corner of the piece seem weighty and human. The artist signals the spiritual significance of this moment with a subtle halo. The viewer's sympathy is drawn to the kind and age-lined face of Joseph, who looks right out of the painting toward us.

Zechariah was filled with the Holy Spirit and prophesied:
"Praise be to the Lord, the God of Israel,
because he has come to his people and redeemed them.
He has raised up a horn of salvation for us
in the house of his servant David
(as he said through his holy prophets of long ago),
salvation from our enemies
and from the hand of all who hate us—
to show mercy to our ancestors
and to remember his holy covenant,
the oath he swore to our father Abraham:
to rescue us from the hand of our enemies,
and to enable us to serve him without fear
in holiness and righteousness before him all our days.
And you, my child, will be called a prophet of the Most High;
for you will go on before the Lord to prepare the way for him,
to give his people the knowledge of salvation
through the forgiveness of their sins."

Luke 1:67–77

The priest Zechariah had been struck silent when he did not believe the Angel Gabriel's promise to him that his wife Elizabeth would have a son in her old age. But after John the Baptist was born, Zechariah wrote on a tablet: "*His name is John.*" Straightaway he was able to speak again, he was filled with the Holy Spirit, and his words are captured in this song. Just three months earlier Elizabeth had been filled with the Holy Spirit and had recognized Jesus as her "Lord" in Mary's womb.

Zechariah now emerges from the months of silence during Elizabeth's pregnancy, and he sings a song that has come to be known as the *Benedictus.* The majority of this song is not taken up with his hopes for his own son John the Baptist; he is far more concerned with the salvation that the coming Messiah is going to bring. Mary's son is the inspiration for his song. Only this phrase in the entire song even refers to John the Baptist specifically:

> *And you, my child, will be called a prophet of the Most High;*
> *for you will go on before the Lord to prepare the way for him,*
> *to give his people the knowledge of salvation*
> *through the forgiveness of their sins*

Zechariah prophesies that John the Baptist will go before the Lord to prepare his way by calling the people to repentance. The rest of his focus is on the significance of the coming of Jesus and his over-brimming confidence in God's salvation. Zechariah is a changed man. He has moved from cynicism, doubt, and fear to faith-filled hope. He begins his song: "*Praise be to the Lord, God of Israel, because he has come to his people and redeemed them.*" When we first heard of him, this priest Zechariah could not bring himself to believe that his prayer had been answered—even when the Angel Gabriel appeared to him in the temple and spoke a promise to him that his wife Elizabeth would have a child. Now, Zechariah is filled with the Holy Spirit and he is so confident of God's redeeming work in the coming Messiah that he speaks about it in the past tense. He has absolute trust in the redeeming work of God through the promised savior. He knows that his wife's relative Mary is carrying a child and he is confident that God has visited and redeemed his people in that child. With conviction and faith, the promised act of God is for Zechariah as good as done.

Zechariah lands his song in the hope for the Messiah to bring light in the darkness.

because of the tender mercy of our God,
by which the rising sun will come to us from heaven
To shine on those living under darkness
And in the shadow of death
To guide our feet into the path of peace. (Luke 1:78–79)

His words speak about "*the tender mercy of our God*" for those living under darkness. These poignant words are particularly meaningful for us in the season of Advent. We may feel the sting of loss, grief, and pain at this time of year. Perhaps we remember loved ones lost, or reflect on as-yet unfulfilled hopes, or notice the disappointments of the year that has passed. Jesus the savior has come to shine light for those living in darkness and the shadow of death. This is a reference to the Messianic prophecy of Isaiah. Mary's son was born as a fulfillment of that hope, a light on the horizon for people like you and me. People who walk in darkness—through trauma, devastation, disappointment, or a loss of hope. The prophet foresaw a time when the people walking in darkness would see a great light. Isaiah goes on to say:

> *The people walking in darkness have seen a great light…*
> *For to us a child is born,*
> *to us a son is given,*
> *and the government will be on his shoulders.*
> *And he will be called*
> *Wonderful Counselor, Mighty God,*
> *Everlasting Father, Prince of Peace.*
> *Of the greatness of his government and peace*
> *there will be no end.*
> *He will reign on David's throne*
> *and over his kingdom,*
> *establishing and upholding it*
> *with justice and righteousness*
> *from that time on and forever.*
> *The zeal of the Lord Almighty*
> *will accomplish this.* (Isaiah 9:2, 6–7)

This description of Jesus was given to the prophet Isaiah over seven hundred years before his birth. But at Advent we can look to Mary's son—the child given to all of us—and recognize him as the Wonderful Counselor, Mighty God, Everlasting Father, and Prince of Peace. A light shining for us.

PRAYER

Christ be with me, Christ within me
Christ behind me, Christ before me
Christ beside me, Christ to win me
Christ to comfort me and restore me.
Christ beneath me, Christ above me
Christ in quiet, Christ in danger
Christ in hearts of all that love me
Christ in mouth of friend or stranger.

Prayer of St. Patrick

Naming of Saint John the Baptist. Sano di Pietro (1450–1460)
Metropolitan Museum of Art, New York.

This picture originally formed part of a predella (a small set of panels showing narrative themes under a larger painting on an altar). The image shows two incidents from the life of John the Baptist. In the background, Elizabeth, having just given birth, lies in bed, while her infant John is being cared for by a midwife and friend. In the foreground is the animated face of Zechariah, carefully indicating "his name is John" and then bursting into song and prophecy. Despite the grand setting and style, the artist is at pains to paint an intimate glimpse, with the bed shielded on two sides and a small fire in the grate. The viewer is invited to see a human, private, and personal perspective of these public events.

Now there was a man in Jerusalem called Simeon, who was righteous and devout. He was waiting for the consolation of Israel, and the Holy Spirit was on him. It had been revealed to him by the Holy Spirit that he would not die before he had seen the Lord's Messiah. Moved by the Spirit he went into the Temple court…Simeon took him in his arms and prayed.

Luke 2:25–28

Simeon was a Godly man who lived through the occupation of his land, and with other people of prayer waited quietly and patiently upon God—hoping for the salvation the Messiah would one day bring. The text says that he was "*waiting for the consolation of Israel.*" This phrase gives us a sense of how profound and deep Simeon's grief was over the state of the world. Here was a person of prayer and profound faith who was hoping for God to intervene. After the birth of Jesus, Joseph and Mary brought their infant baby Jesus to Jerusalem when he was forty days old so that they could make a sacrifice required by the Law of Moses (Leviticus 12:1–8).

The details in this story are fascinating—many scholars believe that Luke spent significant time researching his gospel with Mary the mother of Jesus—so we know for example that

Mary and Joseph were relatively poor, as they did not offer a lamb but "a pair of turtledoves or two young pigeons."

As this poor couple come into the Temple, they meet an old man named Simeon—a man who had spent his life in prayer, in worship, and faithful expectation of the day when God would comfort his people. God had promised Simeon at some point in his life, through the power of the Holy Spirit, that he would not die without seeing with his own eyes the Messiah—the anointed King. On that very day he had felt moved to go into the temple.

When he saw the family, Simeon took the child in his arms. This is a noteworthy detail—a new mother remembers the moment a stranger takes her child in his arms. But what Simeon said is even more memorable than what he did. Simeon proclaims that this child is God's salvation for Israel and for the Gentiles. This was another confirmation of what Mary already knew. But the clarity of Simeon's words and the location in the Temple of God caused Mary and Joseph to marvel. But then Simeon turned to Mary, and, having blessed the family, he spoke to her specifically warning her that: "*a sword will pierce your own soul too.*" The suffering of Jesus and the consequent suffering that Mary his mother will experience are starkly prophesied.

We do not know whether Simeon knew of the details of Jesus's birth—the star, the journey to Bethlehem, the manger, the angels, and the Magi—perhaps he had heard something about this baby through the testimony of the shepherds or from someone else. But in God's perfect timing, led by the Holy Spirit, he is in the right place at the right time in order to meet the holy family in the temple. There is no equivocation or doubt in Simeon's mind—this is the moment that the rest of his life has been about—he has longed for the Messiah to come, and he sees in the child Jesus the focus of his hopes and longings.

Simeon took the child in his arms. As a mother myself I remember feeling uneasy about people wanting to hold my babies in the early days unless they were close family members or friends. How must Mary have felt as this elderly man took her baby? But this baby was no ordinary child—and Mary knew that truth. Perhaps she anticipated the prophets' recognition of divinity in her child. But Simeon broke into praise—and declared a prophecy later known as the "Song of Simeon" or the *Nunc Dimittis* (from the Latin for "now dismiss") and still sung by choirs and congregations all over the world in the evening before going to sleep. "*Sovereign Lord, as you have promised, you may now dismiss your servant in peace. For my eyes have seen your salvation which you have prepared in the sight of all nations; a light for revelation to the Gentiles and the glory of your people Israel*" (Luke 2:29–32).

In the baby Jesus, Simeon recognized that the Messiah had come and that he could see him with his physical eyes. And so he was able to say publicly that he was now ready "*to depart this life in peace.*" This is an extraordinary thing for a new mother to hear. In that moment Simeon is so happy that he is ready to die.

What has he seen in this child Jesus? In Jesus, Simeon saw immediately that salvation had come: "*For my eyes have seen*

Your salvation" (Luke 2:30). Simeon recognized Jesus as the One who would bring salvation to humanity. In a culture that revered age and learning—this is utterly revolutionary—an old man pays homage to a baby and calls him God's savior for the world.

In Jesus, Simeon saw that the prophecies of the Old Testament were being fulfilled: "*You have prepared in the sight of all nations*" (Luke 2:31). The Old Testament was a text that was known by the nations of the world around Israel. People knew of their hopes and expectations of a Messiah. Simeon here declares that the time has come for the fulfillment of those promises.

In Jesus, Simeon saw that the light was for everyone. He recognized in that moment that Jesus was not only a savior for Israel but for the whole world—"*A light for revelation to the Gentiles*" (Luke 2:32). Simeon grasps something profound about Jesus here that even the disciples struggled to realize. But in that moment of revelation as he holds the Son of God in his arms, he sees the truth. Simeon also saw in Jesus that this child was the glory of Israel—"*The glory of Your people Israel*" (Luke 2:32).

Simeon is holding the Son of God in his arms, and he is able to recognize who Jesus really is. He has prophesied that Mary's own heart will be broken, but for him, encountering Jesus means that he is ready to die in peace.

PRAYER

Sovereign Lord, as you have promised,
you may now dismiss your servant in peace.
For my eyes have seen your salvation which you
have prepared in the sight of all nations;
a light for revelation to the Gentiles and the
glory of your people Israel. Amen.

Luke 2:29–32

Rembrandt, *Simeon's Song of Praise*, Mauritshuis,
The Hague, The Netherlands.

As often is the case in Rembrandt's studies, this Dutch master considers Christ to be the Light source of the painting. In this picture, the raptured, energized Simeon contrasts with the peaceful acceptance captured in the demeanors of Mary and Joseph. Everyone listens with attention to the words of promise, including the prophetess Anna, whose face we do not see as the old man's face reflects joy, bathed in the glow coming from the infant Christ. At a distance, sitting up the stairs, are shrouded groups of scholars and priests, clothed in the dark browns and black that teachers were prone to wear in Rembrandt's own day. The painting from 1631 is one of several in which he explored Anna and Simeon in the temple.

*There was also a prophet, Anna, the daughter of Penuel, of
the tribe of Asher. She was very old; she had lived with her
husband for seven years after her marriage, and then was a
widow until she was eighty-four. She never left the temple
but worshipped night and day, fasting and praying. Coming
up to them at that very moment, she gave thanks to God and
spoke about the child to all who were looking forward to the
redemption of Jerusalem.*

Luke 2:36–38

After Simeon's words about Jesus in the temple, an old
lady named Anna comes up to Mary. Anna was an
elderly lady having been widowed after only seven
years of marriage. Now we meet her at the age of eighty-four
after she had dedicated her entire adult life to worshipping God
in the temple "*day and night,*" fasting and praying. It is noted that
she "never left the temple." She was a woman of extraordinary
self-denial and passionate commitment. As a widow she would
have experienced genuine hardship in life, but her response was
to dedicate herself completely to God. She lost everything her
culture valued—her status as a wife, her potential to be a mother,
her financial security, and her home. She lived a life of widowhood, which implies a life of lament and hardship. When she

sees the child Jesus being brought into the temple and when she hears Simeon's words to Mary, particularly his phrase about a sword piercing her soul, Anna is drawn to Mary. A woman who has suffered recognizes another woman who is going to experience profound suffering.

As the story unfolds, we are told in the text exactly who Anna is. We know her father's name (Phanuel), her tribe (Asher—one of the northern tribes of Israel), and her age. She is eighty-four and "very old." These details are important. Anna was an identifiable person, and we are being reassured that the testimony we are reading is evidenced and robust. Anna was a person who lived in a critical moment in history, and she got to bear witness to something earth-shattering as the eternal God stepped into space and time in the person of Christ.

Upon meeting the holy family, Anna gives thanks to God and she begins to speak about Jesus to everyone who will listen. The focus of her words is the redemption she believes Jesus will bring.

Mary takes careful note of this encounter with Anna; she remembers it and makes sure to include it in her testimony to Luke. Why? Mary knew that Jesus was no ordinary child; she understood that he was going to be the savior of the world in some way. But this encounter with Anna must have stood out to her, after the warning from Simeon of her own suffering to come. The sword will pierce Mary's soul. In the very moment that she is hearing of her own coming suffering, Anna laid eyes on Jesus and resonates with the profound suffering that Mary is going to endure. Mary may have felt overwhelmed by what she heard from Simeon. Mary reported to Luke that "the child's parents marveled at what was said." In that moment of marveling and overwhelm, Anna prayed. Her eloquence in prayer is striking. No doubt she would have built credibility in all those decades of presence in the temple, but in this moment her integrity and faith minister to Mary.

For Mary this is a woman who sees her and who takes note of her suffering that has been prophesied as coming. Anna was a woman who had suffered loss herself, and she chooses to come close to another woman whose suffering will be related to her child redeeming the world.

Today any of us who are experiencing suffering or lament during Advent can take heart from the truth that Mary's son has been born into a world like ours. A world in which we may well experience sorrow, loss, and death and yet a world into which the savior has come. And because of him an old woman who has lost out on so many things we take for granted—opportunity, potential, education, security, family, and reputation—is given the role of witnessing the redemption of the world and the opportunity to comfort Mary. The connection between Mary and Anna is forged in a moment of profound recognition. It is unsurprising that Mary treasured this memory. The age difference between the two women was no barrier. Their bond is forged in suffering. Anna joins Mary as a female witness to the Messiah.

Dorothy L. Sayers notes how this is to be a feature of Jesus's ministry—that his core identity is primarily witnessed by women: "Perhaps it is no wonder that the women were first at the Cradle and last at the Cross. They had never known a man like this Man—there never has been such another."[1]

Anna receives a wonderful reward for her faithful service—she gets to see the Messiah with her own eyes. She also gets the honor of being one of the first evangelists recorded in the gospels—as she proclaims the redemption that Jesus will bring. She "*spoke about the child to all who were looking forward to the redemption of Jerusalem.*"

Throughout her years of praying and fasting, in the sorrow of her widowhood, could Anna have realized the significance of her life? She had no children—could she have known that future generations (including us) would know her name and remember her? In the sorrows of her life and all the tragic circumstances Anna experienced, she would not have known this. Yet she gets a front-row seat on the redemption of the world. God rewards her years of faithfulness. And Anna encourages Mary and points those who suffer in sorrow and lament to the one who was born to redeem the world through his own suffering.

---

1   Dorothy L. Sayers in *Unpopular Opinions* (London: Victor Gollanz, 1949), p. 122.

PRAYER

Almighty and ever living God, we humbly pray that,
as your only-begotten Son was presented in
the temple, so we may be presented to you with
pure and clean hearts by Jesus Christ our Lord;
who lives and reigns with you and the Holy Spirit,
one God, now and for ever. Amen.

The Church of England Book of Common Prayer

Rembrandt, *The Prophetess Anna*,
Rijks Museum, Amsterdam.

In 1631, The Dutch painter Rembrandt created this master-piece. The artist is known for his atmospheric use of light and dark, and here he bathes Anna in light. She is shown poring over the well-worn Hebrew scriptures, in expectation for the Messiah and looking for the fulfillment of prophecy. Light floods in from the left, and then reflects off the pages of scripture to give a warm glow to the lined face of this prophetess. Many modern portraits celebrate the young, but Rembrandt took most pleasure in more elderly subjects, giving their faces a dignity appropriate to their years and pathos for their experiences. He celebrates wisdom and character in paint. Anna sits, without slumping on a stool, energized by what she reads, almost leaning forward in longing for redemption.

After Jesus was born in Bethlehem in Judea, during the time of King Herod, Magi from the east came to Jerusalem and asked, "Where is the one who has been born king of the Jews? We saw his star when it rose and have come to worship him."

Matthew 2:1–2

The Magi were known figures of historical significance at the time. They are mentioned in other contemporary texts. They came from Mesopotamia. The Magi were a known part of the ruling elite of the Parthians at the time Matthew is describing—they had religious, astrological, and philosophical learning and they were also political figures. Some of the Magi were Parthian diplomats who were interested in foreign leadership and governance. The Greeks and Romans knew the Magi as part of the ancient world elite. And it is a group of Magi who arrive to pay respects to Jesus Christ after his birth. Mary had experienced confirmation of the truth of the incarnation in the birth of Jesus from the Angel Gabriel, Elizabeth, a group of shepherds, Simeon, Anna, and now Magi.

First of all, they go to the court of Herod, having logically deduced that this was the most likely place of a king of the Jews to be born. A group of Parthian Magi turning up to visit

Herod would have been politically and religiously significant. Magi were famous in the ancient world for getting their astrology right. And the historian Josephus tells us that Herod was interested in signs and omens. Now this group arrives and tells him a new King of the Jews had been born. They would have had enormous credibility with Herod. These men are learned stargazers, well used to deducing philosophy from the night sky, and based on what they see, they arrive in Jerusalem looking for a child who has been born King of the Jews. They have seen evidence, and based on that they decide to seek out this child to worship him.

The psalmist tells us that "*the heavens declare the glory of God*" (Psalm 19:1). It is not unusual for people to find their way to Christian faith through studying cosmology and astronomy. Alister McGrath studied the stars as a teenager, and this awakened in him the possibility of God. He writes:

"Back in the 1960s, we were told that religion was fading away, to be replaced by a secular world. For some of us that sounded like a great thing. I was an atheist back in the late 1960s, and remember looking forward to the demise of religion with a certain grim pleasure. I had grown up in Northern Ireland, and had known religious tension and violence at first hand…The future was bright and godless…I started out as an atheist, who went on to become a Christian. I had originally intended to spend my life in scientific research, but found that my discovery of Christianity led me to study its history and ideas in greater depth. I gained my doctorate in molecular biophysics while working in the Oxford laboratories of Sir George Radda, but then gave up active scientific research to study theology."[1]

But the Magi's belief, deduced from the star they have seen, is more specific than a belief in God. There have been many explanations as to what this star might be. Some have suggested that the Bethlehem star was a supernova, a comet, a massing of planets, or the conjunction of Jupiter and Venus on June 17, 2 BC. It could be that any of these explanations are the right one, or perhaps the star was a supernatural phenomenon placed there by God, since the star Matthew describes appears to be dynamic; after all it *"went ahead of"* and *"stood over where the child was."*

The star somehow alerted the Magi to Christ's arrival, inspiring them to leave everything, and travel east to Jerusalem. This shows us something very significant about Jesus. Although Jesus was born in relative poverty and humility to an unmarried mother who was part of an oppressed people living under Roman occupation, these eminent, powerful, scholarly men have discerned from the evidence that one who is worthy of their worship has been born.

Light observed in the heavens has attracted them to worship the one they believe has been born a King of the Jews, and following the constellation or star, they find Jesus with Mary. And they worship him. This is as astonishing in that culture as

---

1   Alister E. McGrath, "Loving Science, Discovering God: An Autobiographical Reflection on Science and Theology," *Theology & Science* 17 (2019): 431–443.

in ours today—for men with great influence and power to kneel and worship a baby.

The Magi, with all of their philosophy and scientific learning, recognize that this child is worthy of their worship. And they offer him gifts. Three are mentioned in particular. Gold for kingship. Frankincense, which was key to the role of priest, signifying holiness. And myrrh, a spice used in burial. An unusual gift for a baby, but Jesus is no ordinary baby; his death will be sacrificial, and the myrrh points us to the meaning of his death. They provide us with a beautiful and rare image of power. They are prepared to humble themselves and use their power to kneel in worship of the true King.

But Mary's world is also a world where power is corrupted and corrupting. Herod is a megalomaniac ruler, a deceptive and dangerous character with an active religious veneer. This powerful man even pretends to want to worship the newborn King of the Jews, but he has no such intention. He hopes to crush any threat to his own position. Herod is a consummate and brutal power abuser.

When Herod realizes that the Magi aren't coming back to see him after they have found the child, and that they aren't going to show him the way to the baby born to be King of the Jews, he decrees that all the boys under two years of age in the Bethlehem area be slaughtered. This is the kind of man Herod was—perfectly capable of murdering young children, one of whom was a potential threat to his kingship. Ancient sources tell us that on his deathbed, Herod realized that the Jews would celebrate, not mourn, his death. To ensure that the

Jews mourn when he died, Herod commanded various Jewish nobles be murdered—so that as their families mourned there would be a period of mourning after his own death.

The gospels do not flinch from describing reality even as we think about Jesus coming as the light of the world—darkness is real. What a contrast with the light of the star, and the joy of the Magi who humble themselves before the baby of Bethlehem!

At the turning of this year, in Advent, we may feel surrounded by darkness, anxiety, lament, and fear—but there is hope. With the Magi can we discern the signs? The signs are there for each of us to see too. The star or constellation signifying the birth of the King of the Jews in Bethlehem, the prophecies in the Old Testament about Jesus's life and birth. The Magi recognize, when they find the mother and her child, that Mary's child is worthy of their worship. Isaiah 60 speaks of kings coming to the brightness of the Lord's dawn and light, and this is an invitation to us to do the same. In this dark world why not invite the light of the world to shine upon us today?

PRAYER

Heavenly Father,
whose children suffered at the hands of Herod,
though they had done no wrong:
by the suffering of your Son
and by the innocence of our lives
frustrate all evil designs
and establish your reign of justice and peace;
through Jesus Christ your Son our Lord,
who is alive and reigns with you,
in the unity of the Holy Spirit,
one God, now and for ever. Amen.

The Church of England Book of Common Prayer

Bruegel, *The Adoration of the Kings*,
The National Gallery, London.

Pieter Bruegel the elder, and his son, Bruegel the younger, both returned to this subject of the adoration of the Magi several times. They placed their subjects in a crowded scene translocated to the Flemish countryside, so familiar to their viewers. This painting, from 1564, draws on the Italian custom of closer perspective and more staged settings. The artistic tradition typically explored the global impact of the Magi, depicting them as coming from the three known continents of the time—Europe, Asia, and Africa—but also showing three ages: young African, middle-aged European, and elderly Asian. The gifts are ornate and precious, with gold presented as a finely worked boat, with an intricate miniature monkey climbing out of an emerald shell to grasp at an inlaid sapphire. The church feast of the Adoration, which celebrates this encounter, was January 6, and this celebration marked the end of the twelve days of Christmas, which is why this painting was contextualized to the weather with Mary wearing fur lining, Joseph with a hat, and onlookers wrapped up against the cold. Meanwhile the agitation of soldiers and onlookers reminds us that the birth of Christ did not occur at a time of peace and that his life would be marked by the turbulence of crowds and rulers, ultimately leading to his crucifixion. Jesus's death is signaled in this painting of his earliest days as a rugged cross beam is visible above their heads, and the child appears to be wrapped in a shroud as in the day of his death. The picture was painted with a backdrop of war in the Flemish region; perhaps this painting can be seen also as a prayer for Peace.

While they were there, the time came for the baby to be born, and she gave birth to her firstborn, a son. She wrapped him in cloths and placed him in a manger, because there was no guest room available for them. And there were shepherds living out in the fields nearby, keeping watch over their flocks at night. An angel of the Lord appeared to them, and the glory of the Lord shone around them, and they were terrified. But the angel said to them, "Do not be afraid. I bring you good news that will cause great joy for all the people. Today in the town of David a Savior has been born to you; he is the Messiah, the Lord. This will be a sign to you: You will find a baby wrapped in cloths and lying in a manger."
Suddenly a great company of the heavenly host appeared with the angel, praising God and saying,
"Glory to God in the highest heaven,
and on earth peace to those on whom his favor rests."
When the angels had left them and gone into heaven, the shepherds said to one another, "Let's go to Bethlehem and see this thing that has happened, which the Lord has told us about."
So they hurried off and found Mary and Joseph, and the baby, who was lying in the manger.

Luke 2:6–16

Thy time came for the baby to be born. Today is the day that Christians all around the world celebrate the birth of Christ. And we see in this extraordinarily intimate narrative what happened. Every woman who has had a baby has their own birth narrative. I can think of all sorts of details of my own experience of giving birth to my children. And here we have Mary's detailed insight into the birth of Jesus. Don't skip over the wonder of that truth. Mary's account includes little details that mattered greatly. She wrapped her baby in swaddling clothes and placed him in a manger.

We may have an idealized view of the baby in the manger from store windows at Christmas, or from beautiful paintings. But a manger was an animal feeding trough. Mary was not at home in Nazareth; she and Joseph had traveled to Bethlehem for a tax census. The place where they were to stay did not have a separate room, so they find themselves needing to use a manger for the baby to sleep in.

A profoundly theological point is being made. As a new mother, needing to place her newborn son in an animal feeding trough would have stood out to her; that would have been a memorable detail to any parent. But the manger takes on a greater significance as the story continues.

There are shepherds who are at work overnight out in the fields, and they're watching over their flocks in order to protect them from predators. As they are carrying out their normal working lives, angels appear in the sky over the fields. The angels are stunning, and the glory of God shines around them. The angels have a message for the shepherds. *"Today in the town of David, a savior has been born to you; he is the Messiah, the Lord."* Being down-to-earth types, the shepherds need some convincing. And they are told, *"This will be a sign to you. You will find a baby wrapped in cloth and lying in a manger."*

The very detail that was unusual and significant to Mary as a new mother in her birth narrative of laying her child in a manger actually becomes a sign to the shepherds that this is God's Messiah. This is the Lord of all who has been born, and a sign that can help them know which baby that was recently born in Bethlehem is that this particular child will be lying in a manger wrapped in cloths.

In Mary's very great vulnerability as a new mother and in her openness about that detail of needing to lay the child in the manger, a deep truth about who Jesus is emerges. Jesus is the Son of God, and his birth is accompanied by angelic hosts appearing and worshipping and shining in glory. And Jesus is God with us. God is born as a baby into the vulnerability of this world, where men work on night shifts looking after sheep in order to protect them from predators or theft, where families are displaced by the movement of people at the behest of tax officials, and where a young person becomes a mother for the first time, laboring in an unfamiliar place. Jesus is Immanuel—God in all his glory, heralded by angels, with us—in our world, where things can feel dark, vulnerable, and uncomfortable.

Today whether we find ourselves in a season of plenty or poverty, remember who Jesus is, who he came for, and that his first cradle is a sign of God with us.

Blessing: May you be filled with the wonder of Mary, the obedience of Joseph, the joy of the angels, the eagerness of the shepherds, the determination of the Magi, and the peace of the Christ child. Almighty God, Father, Son, and Holy Spirit bless you now and forever. Amen.

PRAYER

Lord Jesus Christ,
your birth at Bethlehem
draws us to kneel in wonder at
heaven touching earth:
accept our heartfelt praise
as we worship you,
our Saviour and our eternal God.
May God, who has called us out of darkness
into his marvellous light,
bless us and fill us with peace. Amen.

The Church of England Book of Common Prayer

Botticelli, *The Mystical Nativity*,
The National Gallery, London.

Sandro Botticelli, who painted this picture in 1499–1500, creates an uncrowded scene of the birth of Christ. He manages to incorporate twenty angels, the Magi, some shepherds, a few fleeing demons creeping into the rocks, and the holy family framed by a simple stable with animals also present. Florence, Italy, at the turn of the millennium was in turmoil. A religious revival under a monk named Savonarola had turned the city on its head, with many reconsidering their opulent and decadent lifestyles, disposing of their distractions in the original "bonfire of the vanities." The foreground depicts an echo of Jacob wrestling an angel, as three men wrestle angels, becoming progressively overcome from left to right, even as they try to resist the progress of God. The inscription at the top of the picture draws attention to the year of the painting, and the opening of a new century. The verse of scripture from the book of Revelation is placed in the heaven opening up at the top of the painting; this emphasizes an immediate call to respond to Christ as the year draws to an end around Christmas and a new year begins. The artist calls us to heed the advice of two angels who counsel five simply clothed figures who are kneeling so that the viewer is also urged to join and recognize the significance of the coming of the Messiah and worship him.

AFTERWORD

We began this journey of *Mary's Voice* by imagining what it would be like to be a young woman in a forgotten corner of an occupied country oppressed by a powerful empire. This woman lived at a time when a woman's voice meant nothing, and yet she went on to have a global impact on the subsequent history of the world.

Despite her lack of formal education, Mary's theological contribution as a witness and theological reflector should not be underestimated. Her eyewitness testimony to Luke, in particular, captured the details of the events surrounding the incarnation of God in history. Mary's knowledge of the Old Testament and reflection upon the meaning of the events she participated in enable us to truly see Christ and to wonder at the beauty of his redemptive plans for the world.

Mary's testimony is recorded and preserved for us, but so are her words. Her song, the Magnificat, draws on the truths of the Old Testament and prophesies what the ministry of the Messiah, her son, will be like. Mary's words form the basis of Christian ethical teaching, and her song has been used in worship by the global church since the earliest days of Christianity.

Mary is the only person to be present with Jesus at his birth and at his death. She stands as a historic eyewitness in both moments. After all, the gospels note that the male disciples deserted Jesus, and apart from John, they are not mentioned as being present at Jesus's crucifixion. But Mary was present, supported by her sister and by other female friends. Comparison with Mark 15:40 and Matthew 27:56 makes it almost certain that this sister was called Salome, and she was the wife of Zebedee, in which case James and John were cousins of Jesus. *"Standing near the cross were Jesus' mother, and his mother's sister, Mary (the wife of Clopas), and Mary Magdalene"* (John 19:25, NLT).

Mary comforted Jesus as he entered this world as a baby, and also as he left it to return to the Father. Jesus was so moved by his mother's loving presence that during his crucifixion he spoke to her, giving her his closest friend, John, as a son to love her after his own death.

> *When he saw his mother and the disciple whom he loved standing nearby, he said to his mother, "Woman, behold, your son!" Then he said to the disciple, "Behold, your mother!" And from that hour the disciple took her to his own home* (John 19:26–27).

Traditions say that Mary lived the rest of her life with John, either in Jerusalem or accompanying him to Ephesus. But this intimate moment of concern captures the familial and personal love of the son of God for his mother.

What did Mary do with the rest of her life? John's gospel

appears to make a particular point of affirming Mary's role of leadership and significance. At the wedding at Cana, Mary launches Jesus's ministry with her intervention to the servants at the wedding when the wine has run out. Her phrase *"Do whatever he tells you"* instigates the first miracle that Jesus did in his public ministry. During the era when the gospels were written, the first person in a list is often thought to signify the leader of the other people in the list. For example, Peter is listed first among the twelve disciples at Matthew 10:2–4, Mark 3:16–19, and Luke 6:14–16, and he is considered their leader. In John 19:25, however, Jesus's mother is listed first among the women at the cross. She could be listed first because she was his mother, but the authors of the other three synoptic gospels don't do this. John is making a particular point—affirming Mary's role of leadership. In addition, at John 2:12, when they traveled with Jesus from Cana to Capernaum, Jesus's mother is listed before "his brothers" and "his disciples." It seems that the author of John's gospel was deliberate, in positively affirming Mary's role during Jesus's ministry and in twice identifying her as having a form of leadership among the other disciples, both women and men.[1]

Mary continued to point people to Jesus. She used her voice and her gifts to serve the early church. She served as an example of a woman who could lead and speak. A speech attributed to Demetrius, the third-century Archbishop of Antioch, says:

---

1   See Ally Kateusz, *Mary and Early Christian Women* (London: Macmillan, 2019).

"Hail, Mary, through whom and by whom all the women in the world have acquired freedom of speech with her Lord!"[1] The poet Ephrem the Syrian (306–373) wrote: "In Mary there has come hope for the female sex: from the insults they have heard and the shame they have felt she has given them freedom."[2] Another author in the seventh century described Mary in the early church as a liturgical leader "who praised God, preached the gospel, led the prayers, set out the censer of incense to God, healed with her hands, exorcised, sealed, sprinkled water, and gave women evangelists powerful writings, or books, to take around the Mediterranean."[3]

Mary was a witness, a teacher, a leader, and a mother. Her voice mattered to Jesus, and it meant something in the early church.

The portraits of Mary in Christian art and iconography appear to have slowly changed her from being seen as a liturgical leader with arms raised in blessing, proclamation, or prayer to a silent woman who physically expressed her submission by looking at the floor. The demure Mary of Renaissance paintings does not cohere with the woman who defiantly proclaimed in her Magnificat: "*he will bring down the rulers from their thrones.*" But somehow Mary as a silent mother figure became a feminine cultural ideal for women.

---

1   Demetrius of Antioch, *Discourse on the Birth of Our Lord*, 35b in E. A. Budge, *Miscellaneous Coptic Texts* (London, 1915), p. 664.

2   Ephrem, *Hymn on Mary*, no. 2, 10 in Sebastian Brock, *Bride of Light* (Kerala: Gorgiass Press, 1994), p. 36.

3   Kateusz, pp. 79–84.

Mary's own voice says something different. She was a person of courage and faith. A woman who knew the Old Testament scriptures and willingly stepped into a significant role in salvation history. Ultimately Mary always seems to point us away from herself and toward her son—the longed-for Messiah—and in so doing she shows herself to be a witness, an evangelist, a pastor, and a leader. In reflecting on *Mary's Voice* in the Advent season we find ourselves marveling not at her, but at Jesus Christ her beloved son.

For Christ is born of Mary,
and, gathered all above
while mortals sleep, the angels keep
their watch of wond'ring love.
O morning stars, together
proclaim the holy birth,
and praises sing to God the King
and peace to all the earth.
How silently, how silently,
the wondrous gift is giv'n!
So God imparts to human hearts
the blessings of his heav'n.
No ear may hear his coming,
but in this world of sin,
where meek souls will receive him, still
the dear Christ enters in.
O holy Child of Bethlehem,
descend to us, we pray,
cast out our sin and enter in,
be born in us today.
We hear the Christmas angels
the great glad tidings tell;
O come to us, abide with us,
our Lord Immanuel!

Christmas Carol: *O Little Town of Bethlehem*

Cathedral of Cefalu, Sicily, Italy.

In the golden mosaic apse of the Cathedral of Cefalu in Sicily, under a huge depiction of Christ, is a figure of Mary. Jesus is shown as Creator of all things, blessing those who come to worship, and with words from the open page of John's gospel declaring in both Latin and Greek, "I am the light of the world, who follows me will not wander in the darkness but will have the light of life." Below stands Mary, with her hands raised, and eyes forward. She is flanked by four archangels and stands above a row of the gospel writers. The cathedral itself took about a century to build—it was started in 1130—and the mosaic artists were brought from Constantinople and completed the work by 1170. The significance of raised hands and the robes of Mary, especially to the Eastern iconographic tradition from which these images derive, is a lively exploration of her inspirational example as a Christian minister in the early church, rather than as an object of adoration herself.

This book could not have come together without the expert artistic advice of my husband, Reverend Canon Dr. Francis (Frog) Orr-Ewing. Your lifelong love of art and knowledge of the manuscripts of the church have added so much to this work, and I am so thankful for your patience with me as we chose each piece together. Your love and tireless strength have sustained me throughout the writing process of this book and in twenty-five glorious years of marriage.

Thank you to Nancy Gifford for your creative vision, wisdom, and unflagging energy in helping me produce the original ideas that inspired this work. Your friendship and support mean the world to me. Thank you to Rio Summers for your hard work, creativity, and energy throughout the process of imagining and envisioning the series of devotional thoughts underpinning the book.

Thank you to my agent, Joy Eggerichs Reed. Your generosity and encouragement at a critical moment in my life have made all the difference. Thank you to my editor, Jeana Ledbetter, and the team at Worthy. Your attention to detail and the sheer excellence with which you approach your work has been a huge blessing to me.

Thank you to Latimer Minster, my community and church

family, and to the people of Stampwell Farm who love beauty, care for people, and honor the Creator. Thank you to the team at Lambeth Palace Library for your welcome, advice, and help with the manuscript collection.

Thank you to my family—Frog, Zac, JJ, and Benji. You have released me to work and cheered me on, championed me and encouraged me every step of the way. Thank you to faithful friends—for your hospitality, listening ears, and gifts of time and wisdom—Matt and Beth Redman, Tim and Julie Wanstall, Cameron and Caroline Collington, Antje and Simon Ransom, Abi Willets, Julia Manning, Ruth Kennedy, Jo Saxton, Julia Sloan, Lee Cheng, Yong Yeoh Yeow, David Bennett, Mari and Ithai van Emerick, Sarah Yardley, Jasmine Wigglesworth, Hazel Thompson, Ruth Malhotra, Max Baker-Hytch, Lori Anne Thompson, the Yearwood family, and David and Clare MacInnes. Thank you to the survivor friends who have trusted me with your stories and who first helped me to hear the meaning and power of Mary's words of hope in the Magnificat.

ABOUT THE AUTHOR

DR. AMY ORR-EWING is an international author, speaker, and theologian who addresses the deep questions of our day with meaningful answers found in the Christian faith. Amy is the author of multiple books including *Where Is God in All the Suffering?* and the bestselling *Why Trust the Bible?* Over the last twenty years, Amy has given talks on university campuses around the world. She holds a doctorate in theology from the University of Oxford and is honorary lecturer in divinity at the University of Aberdeen.